Are you two sisters?

a memoir
Hester van der Walt

modjaji books

Published in 2019 by Modjaji Books
www.modjajibooks.co.za

Translated by Suenel Bruwer-Holloway

Cover photograph: Hester van der Walt and Lies
Hoogendoorn, Darling Street, Cape Town, *circa* 1970.
Photographer unknown.

Translation copy editing by Jo-Ann Bekker
Book cover text by Jesse Breytenbach
Typesetting Andy Thesen
Set in Garamond

ISBN: 978-1-928215-74-5
ebook: 978-1-928215-75-2

Dedicated to the late Anne Schuster and
Annemarie Hendriksz for bringing books to life

Foreword

To deny your ancestors is to deny yourself. I am they and they are me.

I do not have a separate self. We all exist as part of a wonderful stream of life.

– from *no death, no fear*
by Thich Nhat Hanh

The whistle of a train at Springfontein

the smell of manure rising from the clods
my every cell, my building blocks come from my ancestors
ashamed for so long, afraid of being different
and yet we flow together in the same stream of life

my every cell, my building blocks come from my ancestors
ashamed for so long of where I come from
and yet we flow together in the same stream of life
one stream of life, the flow of what is

once I was ashamed of where I come from
the whistle of a train at Springfontein
one stream of life, the flow of what is
the sound of a fog horn on an autumn morning

the whistle of a train at Springfontein
ashamed for so long, afraid of being different
the sound of a fog horn on an autumn morning
the smell of manure rising from the clods

At the turn off to Breë Street, two pedestrians walk towards our car. The women stare at Lies and me and wave. I look and look again and then I recognise Marian Jacobs, a friend I first met in 1978. The years fall away. I fling open the Toyota's door and we embrace in the middle of the dirt road. The lovely young woman at her side must be Tamlyn, her daughter, whom I last saw when she was about eight years old. They are spending the weekend in McGregor and are staying in a guest house across the road from us.

So the long conversations and the do-you-remembers begin. And what happened to so and so, and did you hear about that, and do you know that Brian died? Within minutes we are as close as we were fifteen years ago, when we saw each other all the time. When Marian was Lies's boss (her kleinbaas – Marian's head barely reaches Lies's armpit) and they both worked at the University of Cape Town's Child Health Unit. Since then Marian has wandered far and wide, an international expert on child health who currently advises the Minister of Health.

A strange pattern develops over the weekend. We remain standing in one spot for long spells, as if talking and marvelling over each other's lives is the only thing we need to do. We forget to sit down, to eat, all we do is catch up. And there is so much catching up to do. Where does one begin?

The mark of true friendship, we realise on Sunday evening when Marian treats us to a grand reunion dinner at a good restaurant with the best wine from our area, is that one can pick up the threads as if they were dropped last week. That and the total absence of reproach, guilt or expectations, such as "I should have told you!" or "But why didn't you tell me?"

I realise again how full my life is now, how rich every life is and how little control we have over it all. And yet every life has its turning points, moments when we make decisions that completely alter the course of our lives. It was such a turning point, thirteen years ago, that prompted me to resign from my job in Cape Town and move, with my life partner, Lies, to the village of McGregor. A few weeks later, our house was on the market, and when it sold the very next Sunday, the reality of our decision hit me for the first time. It was as if we were driven to throw caution to the wind. Lies had retired by then, and I resigned from my job against the advice of financial and professional consultants.

I often wonder about the great turning points in every life. My way of making sense of these musings is to rise early in the morning to write. And that is how this memoir developed. Anne Schuster, my writing guru, presented a virtual Flash Memoir course by e-mail. Over eight weeks I received a task at six o'clock every morning. Every week I mined a new turning-point and retraced my life.

1

Ancestors

"Hmm, she thinks I've gone, but I watch her every morning, this eldest daughter of mine. In this photo I'm barely fifty, much younger than she is now. Odd that a daughter can overtake a mother in age, but of course that's only true in this photograph. It was a publicity picture for one of my plays. She says it is her favourite photo of me. I posed for the photographer, and yet there is something in my expression she likes, something of the real Ma, perhaps a trace of slight hesitation or contemplation. But wait, I am the has-been now. This is about my daughter, my oldest and most pensive child.

"For seven weeks she's risen before five every morning. She rummages around for about an hour collecting warm things. Two or three layers of clothing, an oil heater, and believe it or not, even a hot water bottle for those icy feet that never stay warm on their own. A beanie and gloves. A mug of hot tea, and finally down she sits, swaddled like an Eskimo. She has arranged all her props around her: an alarm clock, a small basket with toys like glue, crayons and scissors. It makes me sorry I never believed in playschool, but it's never too late. There goes the alarm. She closes her eyes for a moment and sits dead still. Thank the Lord, she has returned to the faith! Then she starts scribbling furiously. Why is she in such a hurry? It's not like she has a train to catch. The child doesn't even work anymore. She has all the time in the world. But then she always was driven and focused. And so determined to do everything just right, even when she was so ill, with that chest of hers. I know this writing lark will also turn out well. Perhaps another gold medal?! Not that I would ever say so aloud; it would only exasperate her and ten to one she'd stop writing."

Ja, that's the voice of Debora Rossouw, my late mother, who gazes down at me from the frame of her photograph. Somewhere along the line Ma lost the Deb and became Ora. Was it in Oupa and Oupa's house where you were the tenth of twelve children? The little one in a huge team of older brothers and sisters? You were born in 1919, between the two world wars. How old would your mother have been? Surely at least forty. You and your younger sister Rina grew up together in that bustling household, living first in Wellington and later in the Strand. Oupa Piet, your father, sold vegetables and merchandise; these days he would be called an entrepreneur.

Purple, red and blue glass panels mesmerise me while the minister's voice drones on in the background. I lean my cheek against Oupa's arm. The sleeve of his coat releases a low, dark brown buzzing. I smell the earth on his clothes.

"Why do you still wear this old thing to church?" Ouma wants to know. "The elbows are shiny with age." I don't think he heard her.

Today I know why he wore that coat. One wants to feel comfortable in old age. Get rid of everything that is tight and new, that chafes and constrains. I hear his voice again, always an octave lower when the congregation hit the high notes.

"*To You O God my hymn of thanks, You that I praise at eventide …*"

As a child it was only with Oupa that I knew there was Someone keeping all of us safe: I felt that security alongside Oupa in the church, in his vineyard, on his stoep and kneeling in front of his riempie chair. I think it had less to do with the church than with Oupa's roughened hands, his threadbare coat sleeves and his toothless gums.

My favourite story about my oupa is one of his market day adventures. Once in the Boland, late one summer afternoon, he was travelling home over Sir Lowry's Pass with crates of live chickens on the back of his open truck. On the steep descent, when he wanted to slow down, his brakes suddenly failed. He went hurtling down the mountain at breakneck speed. He kept his head and kept his eyes on the next tight bend in the road. Behind him he heard the crates being flung off the back of the truck on each sharp curve. "And then, Oupa? What happened next?" "And then I got home safely, by the grace of God." At that time I was only worried about the chickens who had been hurled off the cliffs somewhere. But Oupa comforted me with the knowledge that they would probably have lived longer on the mountainside than at the market.

....

On our way home Pa stops at the hotel in State Road. Ma gets upset.

"Ag no, dear! We're all tired. Let's just go home."

Pa pretends not to hear her. He walks around the corner to the bar. "Just one beer," he calls over his shoulder.

We remain seated in the Nash. After an hour we are still waiting. My brothers kick stones on the pavement. Ma wipes away perspiration. Just as she decides to go and fetch him, Pa emerges sheepishly. On the way home he tries to make small talk, but everyone is dead quiet.

Voices from the bedroom. Pa explaining and Ma screaming and crying at the same time. The same old pattern every weekend and on Pa's days off. He was always sober when he had to work and for church on Sundays. He was never violent when drunk, only talkative, repeating the same things over and over until he fell asleep.

Even when Ma was despondent and furious with him, she always told us to remember that Pa was a good man. "Your father's weakness is there for everyone to see. Most of us can hide our sins which is much worse." Still, I was ashamed of him. Of what other people would see. As a teenager, I never wanted to invite friends home. Their fathers were not like mine.

When as a student nurse I studied psychology for the first time, I gained new insights into alcoholism. It's actually an illness, not a sin! A weight fell from my shoulders and I suddenly saw my father with new eyes. On my first visit home I spoke to Ma about it. She was sceptical and dismissive. "No, dear. I've already tried everything. Your father will never change." I even spoke to him directly, but felt we were talking at cross purposes.

Years later when Lies and I were living in Cape Town and Pa was a pensioner, he decided to come and visit us on his own and to travel by plane for the first time in his life. A huge adventure. We collected him from the airport and listened to his stories about the flight. We made a big fuss of him. On the weekend we drove him to Kommetjie and Kirstenbosch and had a meal at a Chinese restaurant he remembered from long ago. Then came the cherry on top: a sunset cruise from Hout Bay to the Cape Town harbour. He and I recalled a trip we took on a fishing boat when I was small.

Later that same visit he became angry with us because we had poured a bottle of brandy down the kitchen drain.

As a child I admired my mother enormously. Especially when we were away from home, at a church function, say, or at school. I saw the way people noticed her, her voice and the way she spoke. Her opinions on things. She was an attractive woman with strong features. Grey-blue eyes and a generous mouth. Quite tall and of medium build. She never paid much attention to fashion. Actually she was ahead of her time, as she liked wearing long pants which she made herself. She and Pa were one of the oddest couples ever! He, frail and reticent. A lift mechanic on a mine. Only talkative after a drink or two, but otherwise quiet and pious. He was a stickler for neatness. He never left the house without a shirt and tie, tailored trousers, a jacket and a hat. Later on he wore a safari suit to work.

Ma often told me about the great love of her life. Wikus from Riversdale. They met just after matric at a Still Bay youth camp. And what happened? She told me that she broke it off because he "wanted to go too far". Much later, when she was twenty-four, she met Fanie, my father, at a dance in Ontdekkers near Krugersdorp where she was nursing. Her younger sister Rina was also there with her Willem, who was Fanie's friend. Fanie immediately fell in love with Ma. She also fell for him, I suspect, even though she found out soon afterwards that he was divorced. She also quickly discovered that he drank too much. It was war time, 1943, so everyone probably drank. But marriage? And producing seven children? That I could never understand. She was in so many ways Pa's superior and his drinking habit caused her endless frustration.

It was only later, while chatting to Lies the "spelunker" who has a way of getting people to talk, that Ma admitted she "had to get married".

I was busy cooking in an open-plan holiday house on a farm in Botrivier. Ma was visiting us for the long weekend. Lies and Ma were drinking tea at the kitchen table and I listened quietly to their conversation while I chopped onions.

"Tell me a bit more about this chap Wikus. He was your first boyfriend, is that right Tannie Ora?"

"Yes. I really loved him."

Silence.

"And then, what happened?"

"He took me to meet his parents in Riversdale. His father was the priest there." Ma's voice grows dreamy. Lies prods her again.

"Ag. Well, it didn't work out."

"Why not, Tannie Ora?"

"He wanted to go too far. And I didn't. I wanted to wait until my wedding night. And so I lost him."

"But later on, with Oom Fanie, then I suppose you didn't hold back?"

I turn ice cold in the silence that follows.

"Yes, my child. You are right," she says quietly. "Then I had to get married. In a magistrate's court."

Now I knew for certain why there was never a single wedding photograph in our home. Nor a date when my parents celebrated their anniversary. And that I was the "cause" of their marriage.

Growing up, I remember my relationship with Ma as being a kind of alliance. She leaned on me, as her eldest daughter. I helped her with the housekeeping and helped to look after the younger children, but I was also her companion. We enjoyed knitting together, sewing clothes, going to the shops and singing in the choir. I helped her make dozens and dozens of koeksisters and pies for church and school bazaars. She admired my achievements at school. She was amazed by my appetite for reading and concerned about my health and the asthma that plagued my teenage years.

And Pa Fanie? He often told us about his tough childhood. After a couple of drinks he would talk endlessly about the hardships of the Eastern Cape stubble fields. He was born in 1909 somewhere near Molteno or Springfontein. His family was dirt poor after the war years. His father, Oupa Fanie, was a share-cropper on a farm and one of a large group of impoverished Afrikaners who found work as stokers on the railways. This meant that Oupa Fanie was frequently shifted from one station to another. Pa's mother died shortly after the birth of his youngest sister. His elder sister had to care for the three younger children and keep house for her father. "You children have no idea how hard life can be," Pa often told us. Then he would talk about walking barefoot for many miles to get to school, often on an empty stomach. He never spoke much about school; as far as I could tell he barely completed primary school, after enrolling at a new school every time they were transferred to another station. As soon as he was big enough to shovel coal, he started working as a stoker with his father and stoked his way up to the Witwatersrand, where he signed up as an apprentice on the mines.

Actually I know very little about my father's life. My silent Pa who only became talkative after a few drinks. And then Ma silenced him. My pa who was so proud of me, while I was so ashamed of him for so much of my life.

I never really knew you, Pa, but I see you more and more in the mirror; in my right ear with its sticking-out flap, in my small, crooked, sensitive feet and hands, and in the hesitant pauses in my sentences when I tell a story. In any company you were always like a stranger. There, but also not there. Pappie, pappa, father, old man. I go through all the names people have called their fathers, but not one suits you, except for Pa. You were always in the background. Skittish. Perhaps preparing for the next assault, like a child that regularly gets beaten.

"What are you doing in the bedroom again Pa? Come and sit with us, love!" They called each other "love", but I never understood it as a term of endearment. Just a habit and sometimes uttered irritably by Ma. He referred to her as "your ma".

I am heartsore when I think of the two of them. There was nothing light or joyful between them. And yet she was good to him in her way. Motherly. Lenient. Out of love? Out of pity?

Good heavens, seven children and countless miscarriages. Did they ever chat companionably or simply enjoy sharing things and laughing together? Perhaps that was not a priority. Ma had her children, a few woman friends, her singing and, of course, her worries. And Pa? He had his stout: the dark beer that he viewed as a health drink, and his many adventures to slyly obtain and conceal it. His cigarettes and his pipe. He made a ritual of mixing different kinds of tobacco together on the dining room table. Pa worked shifts on the mine, back and forth on his bicycle. I was already in high school when he bought his first car, a second-hand Nash. Ma was dead against the purchase. She never trusted him behind the steering wheel. He was so proud of that car. A macho symbol which never suited his delicate appearance. And then he had his Bible and his church.

I was an adolescent before I realised that Pa had been married before. Aunt Johanna, a loud, dark-haired woman, lived with her second husband in one of the other mining towns. Ma regarded her as common. I also had a half-brother and sister I only met much later.

We had regular contact with Ma's Boland family, but never heard or saw anything of Pa's relatives – except for his father, Oupa Fanie, who lived with us. Ma took care of him in our home till the day he died. A frail, silent, strict old man who kept dusty sweets in his drawer. You had to say thank you before he would give you one.

Oupa Fanie was born in 1883, probably in Molteno. According to the information in the family Bible my brother owns, he was married to Lucia Francina Lessing who was a few years younger than him. She only lived to the age of forty-five and produced four children, of whom my pa was the third. I met the eldest brother, Ben, and one of his sisters, Alida, when I was very young – at Oupa Fanie's funeral. Afterwards we went once to visit Tannie Alida, who lived on a plot in the Molteno district. All I remember is how Ma shuddered at the flies floating in the milk.

When Pa was born, soon after the end of the Anglo Boer War, a large percentage of Afrikaners were destitute or unemployed and still trying to recover from the devastating rinderpest, Kitchener's scorched earth policy and the concentration camps. Oupa found work as a stoker on the railways in the Springfontein area and was often transferred from one railway siding to another. School attendance was infrequent and irregular. The children went barefoot until Oupa ordered shoes for them by post. Hence the corns on Pa's feet! As far as I know, Pa only completed Standard Six. Later he completed an apprenticeship and qualified as a lift mechanic on the mines; a job he did for the rest of his life. He was proud of his work, the responsibility of safely operating the huge elevators that transported people, as well as ore ,underground.

Sometimes it takes a lifetime to gain sufficient experience to understand why you do things or avoid doing them (especially the latter). Sometimes a third party does it for you: That is Lies in a nutshell. She rushes fearlessly across any forbidden threshold and people answer her questions! In her inimitable way she lured Pa out of his corner with her attention. Like the day he allowed her to care for his feet. His painful corn-ridden feet. Ma sometimes sent him off to a foot nurse and he was reluctant to undergo anymore pain and suffering.

"No, Oom Fanie. I'm just going to wash your feet and rub some nice ointment into them. No filing and cutting." And with that the two disappeared into the bedroom with a blue basin of water.

The next day I heard Lies ask, "So, how are the feet, Oom Fanie?"

"Nice and comfortable, my dear. We can try the treatment again today!"

....

It was only much later that I came to understand the essential difference between the experiences of the Cape Afrikaners and those who lived further north. Ironically, the first insight came from a book that belonged to one of my fellow inmates in a Pollsmoor Prison cell. I cannot recall the name of the book or the author. I only know that it was written in English, by a South African, and concerned the perceptions and thought patterns of Afrikaners. The deep division between those who trekked and those who remained behind in the colony under the English. And between those who fought and those who collaborated. I began to understand something about the class difference between Ma with her love of languages and music and Pa who tried to hide his inferiority in drink.

2

Childhood

a tiny gap an opening

hands on her knees arms stretched
shoulders hunched up to her ears

she sits on the edge of her childhood bed
as straight as she can to breathe

heart hammering in her head
each gasp for breath laboured

the black and blue capsules
won't help today

what about vicks ma asks
just let me rub your back

at half past four pa returns from night shift
we must get her to a doctor

the child's nostrils flare open and shut
her chest whistles and wheezes

then she coughs up a white plug of phlegm
a round pearl on her tongue

it creates a tiny gap an opening
for breath to come in and breath to go out

thank you thank you thank you trembles her lip
for hope for breath for life

afterwards she sinks back against the pillows
ma's soothing hand wiping her forehead

six-thirty time for school get a move on
ma yells at stefaans and rossouw and lucia

you stay right there, i am taking you to the doctor
the child says nothing just breathes

The whistle in my chest in the middle of the night. Every night when everyone else is asleep I sit bolt upright to breathe. I am afraid Ma will hear me and make a fuss. Prop me up against a pile of pillows and wipe my face with a cold, wet cloth. It is the middle of winter on the Free State Goldfields. Outside, the drone of the mine. That is where Pa works operating huge elevators. Here comes Ma with the sticky red medicine I hate so much. And the doctor's blue and black capsules that make my heart hammer against my ribs.

Later the other children are ready for school, but I am still too shaky to stand. I go over my history homework. "No school for you," Ma says. She gets dressed to take me to the doctor. We walk across the yellow winter grassveld. I close my mouth to keep out the icy wind. Every step a fight for breath.

On a day like today we passed the time away writing love letters in the sand. I dream about Pat Boone. His picture is glued to the inside flap of my schoolbag. His songs leave me weak at the knees. He is so completely unlike the rough school boys. I like Elvis too, but more secretly. Like the forbidden fruit of paradise. I feel clumsy and awkward compared with the other school children. Staffie and her Dawie seem so normal. I suspect I don't belong in a young girl's world. I am in Psalm 130: *Lost in the depths, with no hope of salvation.*

I know I am going to fail matric and study at night to make up for lost time. My heavy schoolbag is filled with books, the history book has black and white pictures of Savonarola and

Cavour. The history teacher is Jan de Klerk, nicknamed The Phantom. I see him in the Reformed Church every Sunday, solemnly taking his place as leader of the elders. I try to remain invisible in his class, but every day he asks me questions, he puts me on the spot. As if he and I have something in common. Because we Doppers know we should excel. He is cold and strict and makes me feel uncomfortable. I know he knows about Pa. And I am ashamed of Pa, of our family. The Phantom is unlike my English and German teachers. I feel they see who I really am. Someone who loves languages and reading.

I knew something was wrong the whole time. Every Monday morning in the school hall we sang *Uit die blou van onse hemel* and the school song *Handhaaf en bou*. And we listened to a sermon. Ja, I knew something was wrong. But what? Was it something to do with the Bantu? We loved Anna who lived in the backyard of our mining house. Ma got angry when other people talked about Kaffirs. She said she would beat us to death if we ever dared insult Anna. In the schoolyard everyone stands and talks in groups. I stick with Ina, now that Staffie and Dawie are inseparable. *Jan Pierewiet, Jan Pierewiet staan stil.* Ma makes me a yellow volkspele dress with a wide petticoat. The tiekiedraai steps make me dizzy. Staffie drags me along with them and I am paired off with Kestell. He is just as shy as me. Black crew cut with a cute cow's lick. And before I know what is happening the two of us are also going out. Sweaty palms and a clumsy open-mouthed kiss. *Afrikaners is plesierig en dan maak hulle so.* I am so scared of missing a step, a turn. I feel stupid when it comes to footwork, to rhythm. Far more at home in the library searching for books to read. I won't dare risk inviting Kestell home.

"Look at you, drunk again!" Ma screams when Pa comes home jolly and talkative in the evening. Her pleading and complaining. Pa's silence. Stefaans's silence. Rossouw and I trying to laugh and play, trying to be normal. What good does it do? I too become quiet at home. Until I wake up in the dead of night with a whistling chest. One thing I know for sure: I must leave here next year.

I remember closing the bathroom door behind me and studying myself in the bathroom mirror. The endless brooding over how I looked. How could I move to a strange place with this face, with such uneven ears; one flat, the other protruding. I remember my stomach churning with nervousness and excitement. After all the dreaming I'm finally getting away from Welkom, away from Pa and Ma's never-ending battles. Away from the shame of a drunken father, a home where the cupboard has no doors. Finally I would have a room of my own where I could leave the light on and read till late without worrying about Lucia and Anetha in the beds beside mine. What would that be like? And what if Ma is right and I'll never be able to do the hard work required of a nurse, with my asthma? "You, always with your nose in a book. How will you manage bed washes, lifting heavy patients and turning them over, the stench and the suppurating wounds?" Ma knew about that life, she had been there, she had to eat the shit of bitchy sisters and difficult patients, but she was made for it and loved nursing. And this quiet, clever daughter of hers? She wasn't so sure.

Even then I knew, deep down, that I was making this choice to get away from Welkom, to get away from mining house number nine in Mitchell Street. The alternative was very vague, but I believed I could do it. I ignored the advice of teachers who thought I was mad. Nursing is for girls who can't study, not for you. I would have loved to go to university like several of my classmates. But my parents had six other children to feed. A bursary? Were there bursaries then? None that I remember.

3

Bloemfontein

Handmade little pottery bowl
you were meant to be round
but turned out skew

nervously my spatula smacks
your wet body into a pentagon
but still you hang heavy on one side
like my mismatched ears

you are an angular curve
defying how circles should behave
I was proud of your light-grey glaze
and the cobalt triangle on every plane
roughly painted on wet glaze
pleasing to the eye
did I know even then that I was skew
not perfectly round
searching for other forms to inhabit
somewhere between angular and curved

what pushed me out the nest?
a longing for space and freedom
I wanted to grow
to find out who I am

January 1962. I sit bolt upright on the edge of my bed in the nurses' home. Washed and dressed in a starched white uniform that stands stiffly away from my body. Cinched at the waist by a white belt, the uniform cuts my torso into two. My legs are encased in nylons, neatly fastened to a suspender belt. The shoes, Dr Watsons, hard and brown and shiny, feel uncomfortable on the sensitive, knobbly feet I inherited from Pa. Last night my feet throbbed with pain after a whole day of standing and walking. Fortunately sleep heals. I read my Bible, the little one with Ma's handwriting on the front page: Micah 6 verse 8. It's the only way I know to summon courage and strength for another day in Ward 17. The sister and seniors know exactly what to do, and they expect me to as well. And then there are the patients who call so urgently: "Bedpan please, Nurse!" I respond as quickly as I can, but sometimes the bed is wet by the time I reach them. I suppose I take too long trying to warm the pan, there isn't much hot water after the morning bed baths.

The terror of the first two weeks was unexpectedly broken by a familiar presence yesterday. When I went to the kitchen to fetch a spoon to feed Mrs De Bruin, I saw a figure I vaguely recognised through the window of the back door. She smiled at me. Tannie Hester! Ma's sister, who lives on a plot outside Bloemfontein, hugged me tightly and immediately my courage and thin layer of self-control crumpled.

I sobbed unashamedly in my aunt's arms. Instantly she became concerned. "Are you sick, child? What is the matter?"

"No, no," I tried to explain. "It's just that …" How could I begin to tell her how scared I was and how hard everything was? I bit my trembling lip to control myself and wiped away the tears. I assured her that all was well and suddenly remembered Mrs De Bruin's food was getting cold, and quickly said goodbye.

Thankfully another half an hour of blessed silence before I have to be in the dining room. I open my diary and write about Tannie Hester's visit. What did she think of my tears? What if she tells Ma how miserable I am? It's just, suddenly I was with someone who knew me, who wasn't going to shout at me. Someone who didn't see me as stupid and clumsy. That's what made me cry, the kindness, the acceptance.

Now that I have grey hair, I look back at my younger self with compassion. She was so defenceless and brave. By then she was already building defences against the worst pain and disillusionment of the grown-up world. Until the sight of a loved one touched her heart and her true feelings poured out. Back then she didn't know about the healing power of tears. Nowadays I cry more easily; although the trembling lip remains a problem, especially in public, but I'm working on it.

I remember the Bloemfontein National Hospital where I finally began to feel at home after nearly four years, although the old wards remained vast and full of terror. I remember the sick people in their blue and pink gowns. The blue blankets and white sheets stamped with the PAO emblem for Provincial Administration of the Orange Free State. The sluice room with its shiny bedpans and urinals and glass beakers for urine samples. Then there were my colleagues. Susan the long-faced girl from Burgersdorp. Green-eyed Queenie, older than the rest of us and worldly-wise, with her smoker's contralto voice. Of the senior staff I remember Sniffles, our nickname for the night matron with her soft-soled shoes, who would suddenly appear behind you ready to sniff out any misdemeanour. Small round spectacles, her hair pinned back under the starched veil. Yet there was gentleness when she talked to patients. They loved her and saw her as a nocturnal guardian angel. The echoes in the long passages. The cling-clang of a falling bedpan. My painful feet in shoes which covered the distance between dining room and ward in record time. The new block with private rooms where Doctor Grundill, the doctor who treated my asthma and other lung conditions, worked.

In those days, nursing was managed by an almost military bureaucratic system, with a strict hierarchy of matrons, ward sisters, staff nurses and student nurses. Each rank was identified by its uniform. Even student nurses had to wear insignia: a white belt with one or two blue stripes for first and second years, a blue belt for third years. I can still see the long hospital corridors cordoned off by double doors. At every door you had to look back and quickly check whether a senior was walking behind you. Then you had to step aside and let her go first, or she could reprimand you and even report you to the senior sister.

My first experience of night duty remains an unforgettable milestone. After my first few months in the women's orthopaedic ward, where by day I was merely a bewildered cog in a large machine, the night duty staff of the same ward was reduced to two, a senior blue belt and me, the junior, responsible for the lives of thirty patients from seven at night to seven in the morning. At midnight we took turns to have a thirty-minute meal break. My salvation was my senior nurse, Nurse Crafford – as thin as a rake, with dark curls, and a soft voice and heart. She was a hero in my eyes, because she could handle any crisis, without blaming anybody or screaming at me or anyone else. She trusted me to do my tasks; she showed me how to give an injection, watched me do it once, and then left me to it. For the first time I felt I might have what it takes to nurse, that I might make a difference to patients. And that realisation helped me keep going, even when my body screamed "no more" and it seemed that morning would never come. For the first time I experienced camaraderie with other colleagues – something that must be earned.

During my second month on night shift my chest closed so tightly that my asthma pump and capsules had no effect. A heavy cold made things worse, and when I reported for duty gasping and wheezing, Nurse Crafford sent me to casualty to see a doctor. After a quick examination and an injection, he admitted me to Ward 8, the ward for staff members. Diagnosis:

bronchitis and asthma. After a few days the infection cleared, but the doctor remained concerned about my asthma and put me on cortisone tablets. An unreal existence. A nurse who is a patient. It gave me time to think about the profession and its thousand-and-one activities. Were the people at home right after all? Perhaps I was not nurse material. But then I thought again about the patients on night shift and the satisfaction I was starting to feel when I knew how to do something correctly and could see it made a difference to the patient.

Every morning at seven when the day shift begins a nurse comes to clean my room. I can see from her belt that she is also a first-year student. I stand beside my bed, in my dressing gown, while she works. She greets me and I notice her Dutch accent immediately. We start talking. She tells me it is her first term at college. They have to work in the wards for an hour a day, before lectures. Lies Hoogendoorn. She reminds me of the Dutch people I met through the Reformed Church in Welkom. The Buters, the Vierbergens and the Kooles. No, she doesn't know them, her parents live an hour away in Edenburg, she explains as she stares at my bedside cabinet. "So many books! Do you read a lot?" she asks, surprised. I help to clear the shelves so she can clean the surfaces with Savlon. The next day she appears at my door again, and we talk some more. She tells me she has just returned from Holland where she also worked in a hospital. I tell her about my concerns about my health, and she encourages me to keep nursing.

By then I had missed nearly three weeks of work and the doctor recommended another two weeks' sick leave. This meant I would miss my group's anatomy and physiology course. The matron reassured me. It wouldn't make a big difference; it just meant I'd do the course a few months later with the next group of students. And so four months later in a new class full of strangers I saw one familiar face. Unmistakable, Lies Hoogendoorn.

She stood out in any group. She moved like a giraffe, elegantly erect, always the tallest woman in the room. She was the tallest girl I had ever met. And so thin! I was shocked when I saw her at the swimming pool one day, her vertebra like a string of beads down her back. Light-brown hair pinned up in a French roll, two hairclips holding her starched white cap firmly in place. Soft summer-brown skin and a profile which reminded me of her ancestors in Rembrandt's paintings. I saw her play the organ one day and noticed her beautiful long fingers. Hands that knew exactly what to do to make a patient comfortable against the pillows. Lies's courage always surprised me. She dared to speak her mind. She seemed unafraid of authority figures who threw their weight around unnecessarily. Especially if they were showing off or talking nonsense. She took no shit from anyone. And she never lied, never even told a white lie. Not as far as I knew, not even to get out of a difficult situation.

It was the beginning of a friendship. What did we have in common? At the time I was just a typical teenager. Well, a serious teenage girl who never took part in the wild adventures of my peers. Fearful, sensitive, idealistic, eager to learn, thirsty for knowledge. Deeply religious. And that was our connection. We were both Doppers, and if we had Sundays off we walked to church together, along the footpath that led to the church in Wilgehof. Hats, stockings and court shoes. Hymn books and Bibles tucked under our arms. Lies visited her sister Corry's family regularly and often invited me along to enjoy the genial atmosphere of a typical Dutch household.

As I got to know Lies, I came to understand her better. She longed for a perfect world without deception. And was easily saddened and disappointed by humankind. She yearned for love, and especially for Leen, a handsome, tall, dark Dutchman who never declared his affections. The bastard toyed with her feelings.

Lies's parents, Oom Gijs and Tante Corry, lived in Edenburg where Oom Gijs owned a bakery. It was an adventure to spend a weekend with Lies and her parents. I had to concentrate hard to understand their Dutch, but with time began to contribute a few words to the conversation. I was overwhelmed by their family culture, so different to mine. Here, without any doubt, the father was the strong leader everybody looked up to. Lies was in awe of him, but I always found him easy to talk to. I was more nervous around practical and organised Tante Corry, who was always busy producing the most delicious dishes for the family. Meals I had to get used to; cabbage stamppot, tomato soups with balletjies gehakt (mince balls). The whole family ate every meal together, at a table covered with a cloth. Tante Corry's motto was "Gewoon drie maal per dag eten, al gebeurd wat ookal!" (Three meals a day, no matter what.) I remember icy winter days in front of the coal stove which burned day and night, and nights on a fold-out bed beneath a pile of thick woollen blankets.

During that time I met Nico, Lies's younger brother. He was the male version of Lies; they had both inherited Oom Gijs's height and strong facial features. Lies's eldest sister Corry resembled her mother, after whom she was named. Nico was passionate about music and interested in any topic under the sun. He was so different to the men I had met before. The silly boys at volkspele and the shy guys at church. Actually, in my four years in Bloemfontein not one man had made an impression on me so far. Couples could meet in the sitting room of the nurses' home – men were not allowed beyond that door – but I avoided it like the plague. Why? I was shy, embarrassed, felt inferior. Those sorts of things weren't meant for me. I did long for love in a vague sort of way, but what I remember most clearly from that time is the feeling that I didn't belong. An outsider. And then Nico appeared. Big, self-confident, Dutch. I saw how he related to his sisters and parents, their easy intimacy and lively conversations at the dinner table. I recall a night of lying wide awake. Amazed, elated, smitten. Too scared to hope or even to tell Lies. Until the day she was cutting my hair in my room in the old wing of the nurses' home. I was sitting on a stool in front of the dressing table while she snipped away. My hair style then? Just long enough to hold the nurse's cap in place with two hair pins. She was probably just trimming the back. She asked how I was, and said she had the feeling I wanted to tell her something. Her fingers stroked my hair and she touched my neck. I felt my stomach churn. Then eventually the words slipped out: "I like Nico ..." Lies was speechless. Nico? Her younger brother? "No man, you don't know him like I do," she said. She knew he had a girlfriend. I swore her to secrecy. But later I discovered that she had indeed told him, and he said we would have made a sorry pair, him with his hay fever and me with my asthma.

Afterwards I often wondered about my short-lived infatuation. In a recent writing exercise I tried to recall what my life tasted like, back then. What were the different flavours? Lies tasted like bread. Not that I would have dreamed of tasting her then, but her friendship was daily sustenance. My crush on Nico was like sherry, the only alcohol I had tasted – almost like communion wine, sweet and full of promise, but fleeting and insubstantial. A wild thrill, without any foundation. Or maybe really based on an unconscious dream, a taste as forbidden as fruit from the tree of the knowledge of good and evil. Had I perhaps transferred my feelings for Lies on to her brother, who looked so much like her?

....

My training in general nursing took three and a half years. I was with my parents in Welkom when I received an overseas airletter from Lies. We had both recently written our final nursing examinations and were due to join a group of colleagues in Cape Town in a few weeks, for maternity training in District Six. Lies wrote that her father had fallen ill on a cruise and had died in Holland. She found it distressing to see her aunts and uncles again at such a sad time. Her mother was trying to be brave, but was too shocked to make any decisions.

I remember the day that Ma and Pa took me to Bloemfontein to offer our family's condolences. Lies and Tante Corry had just returned from Holland where they buried Oom Gijs. An unexpected, shocking end to their long anticipated ocean cruise to Holland to celebrate his retirement. On the ship he suddenly became very ill, and the doctor diagnosed advanced lung cancer. In Gouda he spent his last days in a hospital bed. Lies flew to Holland but arrived only in time to attend her father's funeral and accompany her mother back to South Africa.

The filter coffee Lies's sister Corry serves is a bit too strong for me and I add extra hot milk. Pa says: "No thank you, child. I'd rather have some rooibos tea." Ma sips the coffee reluctantly, but politely. The sun shines through the tall sitting room window with its narrow strip of lace curtain which Tante Corry crocheted. The large anthracite fireplace warms the whole room. After visiting this house for three years, I feel at home in Corrie's living room. But this time everyone is heartbroken. Lies tells how she spent hours waiting at the airport in Rome: "It was terrible. I didn't know a soul. I cried and cried because I knew even then that I would be too late to see him." I try to control my trembling lower lip. I look at Pa from whom I inherited this weakness. As usual Ma takes charge and fills the silence. She puts her arm around Tante Corry: "Ja, I understand, one feels so powerless. But Corry, you must take good care of yourself. It will take time to come to terms with the shock of Gijs's death." Lies's sister is still searching for Pa's rooibos. She has a packet of the tea somewhere, she keeps it especially for Afrikaans visitors.

Lies is thinner than ever with dark rings under her eyes. We walk outside, across the winter lawn. Corry's stripped rose bushes line the brick wall. The sun warms my shoulders. Lies and I walk ahead while our families say their farewells. "It was good to see my Tante Babs again," Lies says. "I told her about our plan to do midwifery in Cape Town with our group. The thing is, I cannot leave my ma alone here in Edenburg. I might be able to go later, with the next intake of students. Tante Babs suggested that I ask you to wait for me …"

She looks at me. Without thinking I say: "Ja of course I will wait for you." Cicadas. The babble of voices. Pa makes small talk with Corry's husband Henk about his old Nash which still holds the road so well. "But once in a while I have to clean the piston rings."

My decision to wait for Lies changed my life. Had I gone to Cape Town with the rest of the group, Lies and I might never have seen each other again. I know now that I exchanged my bond with a larger group of classmates for a connection with Lies. Did I realise that then? I can't recall, but I remember clearly that my reply was spontaneous, I never gave it any thought or asked for time to decide. What does that suggest? That I was already in love? Not consciously, but the word *connection* keeps coming up. And that's exactly what it was; I felt at home with Lies and with her family, and the fact that my family was also present says something. It was probably the first meeting between the two families and it gave our connection even more meaning.

How would my life have unfolded had I decided differently that day? I would have gone to Cape Town with our large group of classmates, and when Lies arrived three months later our friendship would probably have developed further, but perhaps on another level. Or maybe she would have decided to remain in Bloemfontein to be closer to her mother and eventually she would have met the tall dark man of her dreams and had a few children. And me? I would probably have done well in the academic side of nursing and today would be living somewhere in Stellenbosch, in a high-security retirement village with a lock-up garage. A cat on my lap and a balcony filled with pots of geraniums and herbs.

4

District Six

In 1966 I begin my midwifery training at the Peninsula Maternity Hospital in Constitution Street, District Six. I work in Primrose Ward, the antenatal ward, and everything seems strange, so different to the Bloemfontein National Hospital. All the sisters are English and I suspect straight from England, their accents are so unusual.

Today I have to measure and record the blood pressure of three patients every half hour. They have preeclampsia and are heavily sedated in an attempt to keep their blood pressure down. I also have to monitor foetal heartbeats with a black Pinard horn. It isn't always easy, I am still learning to distinguish the sounds. I move the horn all over the women's swollen bellies, concerned that I am hurting them. Then the double doors of the ward burst open and the sister calls: "Quick, all student nurses! Go to Labour Ward to witness a birth!" The three of us drop everything and the sister takes us across the passage to the delivery ward.

The bright light blinds me and then guides my eyes to its focal point, a woman with her knees drawn up high and spread wide apart. The woman is young, perhaps younger than twenty. Her thick black hair is drenched with sweat and plastered to her face. Her eyes are huge and anxious. She is flanked by two sisters, clad in surgical gloves and masks. There is a great deal of noise. Voices talk at the same time. We beginners may watch, but may not get in the way. The senior sister speaks the whole time, giving the mother instructions: "Take a deep breath, breathe out now. Don't push! No, just pant now like a doggie!" The woman takes a breath and someone wipes her face. Finally, with the next contraction, she is allowed to push and it seems to be a huge relief for her. Her perineum is stretched to the limit as the baby's head strains to emerge. I am astonished, as the opening is still no bigger than a coin. Then I see the first black curls of the baby's hair. The nurse wipes away the bloody mucus. Everything between the green sheets looks larger than life beneath the harsh lights. At the next contraction, the sister says, "Now!" First another deep breath, close your mouth and bear down. I see the black slimy little head becoming more visible, the size of a tennis ball now, while the mother's vulva skin is stretched ever thinner. Everything happens quickly now. In the blink of an eye, the sister scoops up the baby's shiny wet body and lays him on the green cloths above his mother's drawn-up knees, away from the blood, mucus and faeces. His eyes are still swollen shut. The mother laughs. All the pain already forgotten, just pure joy when the first shrill cry rises above the commotion. "It's a jongetjie," shouts one of the nurses.

I look down. I hope nobody sees me crying. For the wonder of birth and life. Because suddenly I love my ma more than ever before. How did she do it, seven times over, through such a tiny opening? That evening I write her a letter to say thank you. "Ma," I write, "I never knew giving birth was so difficult." I was the first baby to travel through her most intimate passage.

....

"Nurse! Bring us a baby too!" She is barely knee high, dressed in a pink nightie, wild plaits around her head. The district staff jeep is parked near the Steven Steps and I am walking behind Sister Hoogenhout, carrying the leather suitcase filled with bandages and instruments. It's my first day of rounds as the trainee midwife and I feel strange in the khaki uniform and blue Panama hat that will not stay put in the strong South-Easter. A group of young men stand and smoke in front of one of the rows-upon-rows of semi-detached houses. They greet us and show us where to go. "The baby is just next door, Nursie." The front door is open and we go inside. I smell masala and jeera spices mixed with something strange and sweet. Sticks of colok kemenyan, I discover later, to ward off evil spirits and mask mouldy smells. Our patient, Mrs Mymoena Adams, is lying on a double bed with her day-old baby on a pillow beside her, tightly swaddled in a blue blanket.

We are here to make sure that mother and child are healthy; to check that the mother's uterus is contracting properly and that her vaginal secretions look and smell normal. Any sign of pus is dangerous. During the last two months I learnt all these things in the hospital and lecture room, but it feels very different to practise them here, on a low double bed in the intimate space of somebody's bedroom.

While I examine Mymoena's uterus and breasts, Sister inspects the baby. He begins protesting angrily as soon as she removes his blanket. "But aren't you a cross little man, what are you called?" Mymoena responds: "No Sister, he doesn't have a name yet. The Imam is only coming later this afternoon." Sister removes the bandage, dabs his navel cord with surgical spirits and says it is drying out nicely. Now we wait to see how the baby latches on to his mother's breast. Mymoena slips out her full breast, cleans the nipple with a cloth and the baby's impatient mouth roots hungrily for her nipple. It is her second child and she knows just what to do.

I look around the dimly lit room. The bed is cordoned off by a curtain, behind which two more beds have been wedged in. The whole family share this one room. There is no fresh air and instinctively I start breathing through my mouth. "Do you have time for a cup of tea, Nurse? My Tietie made fresh koesisters for Sunday." Sister says: "Yes, thank you, but it will have to be a quick one." The tea is strong and sweet with a generous dollop of condensed milk. It coats my tongue, but I swallow without blinking; I am Ora's daughter after all. The koeksisters look and taste different to my ma's. Almost like doughnuts tossed in coconut. We drink quickly and then say goodbye because there are many patients waiting. As we leave, I hear a woman's voice singing one of my ma's lullabies.

> Sleep little child sleep
> Outside there walks a sheep
> Lambkin with snowy white feet
> Drinking his milk so sweet
> Sleep little child sleep

And suddenly, like a bolt from the blue it hits me, and I understand what has been worrying me for so long. These people are actually my people. And apartheid is one big fat lie.

....

Spices waft from the kitchen of the Peninsula Maternity Hospital. In those days Muslim patients' families were allowed to bring food from home. Along with the new smells, I learn new words; barishap and jeera. I inhale the salty, fishy air when the wind blows directly from the sea. Then there are the smells of birth; blood, mucus and excrement when the mother bears down. A baby comes into the world covered in a protective white layer called vernix. It looks like a thick, waterproof ointment. The bloody odour of placenta as it is placed in a shiny stainless steel dish. It is my job to rinse every placenta and label each one with the name of the patient. The sister examines my work carefully. I develop the knack of identifying various strong smells when on district rounds. Stuffy houses, the smell of too many people crammed into small rooms. The smell of mould in old houses. Petrol fumes from Sister's jeep. Feeling as if I can't breathe through my nose. Learning to breathe quietly through my mouth when the smells become unbearable. Stuttafords Tea Room's fashionable range of perfumes. Toasted Copenhagens on the balcony overlooking Adderley Street on my day off. The sharp antiseptic aroma of pine trees in Pinelands' Forest Drive. The Parade's odours; heaps of ripe fruit, bokkoms, suurvytjies, samoosas, cinnamon and cardamom. The typical street smells that pervade the city's narrow alleys. Sewage and old rubbish.

We walk out through the hospital's doors, down the steps where a young boy often sits and sings to the nurses. I am amazed by the charm of the area. Of course there are the shacks that feature in the newspapers; the dilapidated houses tilting towards each other. But this place teems with life, there are people on the street from early in the morning until darkest night. The voices captivate me the most. The Afrikaans spoken by the women who come to the clinic is unlike mine, yet I can understand everything. I feel deep affection for a mother whose baby I deliver. My hands are the first to touch her baby. The little body is slippery and wet, straight from her body. We look at each other, the mother and I, and instantly there is a bond between us. Direct eye contact after I spent the night listening to her baby's heartbeat and rubbing her back during every contraction. Through the open window of Primrose Ward I hear the Imam calling the faithful to prayer. At first light, the woman's family comes to visit the baby. The Imam is with them, to bless the little boy. The new grandmother brings her daughter a large bowl of food with a tight lid. I set it aside in the kitchen. The aunt smiles at me: "There is enough breyani for you too, Nursie." When I lift the lid I inhale smells I recognise from all over District Six. So that's what it is! The spices are unknown to my Free State nose, where my ma used

Cartwrights' powder to make curry. I spoon some breyani onto a saucer. Rice, mincemeat, strange green leaves and brown lentils. The taste is a bit strange, but good. Not too strong, yet my whole mouth feels alive. Years later I will learn the names and uses of the spices; barishap, cumin, star aniseed, turmeric, ginger, chilli, garlic and dania. A whole new adventure! And so I learn to smell, taste, feel and listen to the people of Cape Town. They sound a lot like Ma's sisters, who grew up in the Strand. Like family.

During this time I came across a book that was to change my life. Jan Rabie's *Ons, die Afgod.* It begins with a man getting onto a bus and taking a seat at the back. "Then I take a seat beside my brother." The novel awakened me, for the first time, to the cruelty and absurdity of apartheid. Was it only this book? Of course not. By then Lies and her family had often indicated that they found the National Party's policies strange. Stubbornly, I thought, although I didn't often say so aloud, that they did not really know what they were talking about. It took Jan Rabie to make the scales fall from my eyes. Suddenly I looked at everything around me differently. The workers and the patients; people just like us, but second-class citizens. The people with their racy language and repartee. The children in the streets. The newborn babies in the incubators whom I fed every two hours. I looked at them all with care and love, because they were my people too.

It is 1966; the fateful year when bulldozers descended on District Six to flatten people's homes, the so-called hovels, and forcefully move people to God knows where, a place known only as "The Flats". I read the *Cape Times* as well now, it presents a very different picture to *Die Burger.* I am thirsty for more information. And with this new consciousness comes shame. For the first time I am ashamed of my people and their actions. During my first holiday back home in Welkom, I talk to Ma.

I am convinced that if she could see and hear what I have, she would also realise that our political policy is a huge mistake. Ma listens quietly and seems slightly uncomfortable. Then she says reassuringly: "Ag no, my child. Our government knows what it is doing, you don't have to worry about a thing. Everything will turn out fine." Now I am also ashamed of my own family, of my school and of the history lessons stuffed into all Afrikaner children. In matric I even got a B for The Phantom's version of history.

Prime Minister Hendrik Verwoerd is murdered in parliament in September. How does awakening begin? In small steps, I think now, looking back on my life, at the young girl with the asthmatic chest dragging herself up the steep slopes of District Six, amazed at the tablecloth cascading over the mountain. Everything was new to my small-town eyes. I met English people for the first time, a few nurses but mostly sisters, many from England. Initially I found their voices shrill and defiant, until I got to know some of my colleagues better.

That was a year of birth in Cape Town, in more ways than one. I learnt how to be a midwife and was thrown into the deep end of the vital life of District Six. It was wild and exciting, but there were things that made me feel frightened and strange. Things so strange that I did not have words to comprehend the peculiar behaviour of some of the sisters. There were a couple of women who wore men's clothes. I got a big fright when a woman wearing men's trousers and shoes, with a crew cut and huge breasts, caught my eye as she passed by, her arm around the waist of one of the Peninsula Maternity Hospital sisters. When she saw me staring at her, she winked at me. I did not know where to look and quickly turned around and walked straight into someone else. A colleague from Bloemfontein who had already been in Cape Town for a few years, warned Lies and me about these "manly women". She even told us to watch out for them. Them? For all I knew we were like them and the mere thought made me feel scared and ashamed. Lies and I were still friends, still together in these turbulent waters, but those ideas caused a silence between us. We allayed these fears, every Sunday we had free, by catching the train from Mutual Station, near our hostel at Conradie Hospital, to Cape Town Station. From there we walked down Adderley Street, through the Company's Garden to the Reformed Church in Hof Street. We were warmly received and listened to Dominee Stavast with open minds.

Many people from the Netherlands attended the church, and one day we met a Dutch sister from Siloam, the Reformed Church's mission hospital in Venda. I felt warm inside when she spoke about her work. Listening to her, I knew immediately that this was what I wanted to do. Lies chose to go and live with her mother in Bloemfontein and try to find work there.

Who was that person, that younger version of me? She was serious, far too serious for her twenty-two years. Almost unnaturally conscientious, and eager to learn. She was also physically weak and often suffered from serious asthma attacks and bronchitis. Any additional stress exhausted her, and she often had to fight against a small voice warning her that she had chosen the wrong profession.

5

Secrets

Once there was a little girl who wished she could understand English because when her ma and the tannie across the road spoke English they laughed hysterically and sometimes they wept, and she burned with curiosity. So the little girl began to talk to the friend only she could see. Zinn lived under the kitchen table and the two of them made up their own English. Her ma wanted to know who she was talking to. At first she did not want to tell, because it was her very own secret, but, later she did tell her ma. And her ma went and told everybody about Zinn. And so the little girl learnt that secrets are too precious to share. She should rather keep them to herself, or hide them far from view.

....

The train to the north finally stops at Louis Trichardt. I lug my two suitcases into the train's corridor. After Pretoria everything I saw out the window was new. Tall trees, flat-topped mountains. Untamed landscapes. The woman sharing my compartment is also getting off at Louis Trichardt and wants to know where I am headed. "Siloam? Never heard of it," she says. "I suppose it's somewhere in Kaffirland." I keep quiet. That's one thing my ma never tolerated, speaking like that about black people.

It's raining and the small station is muddy. Many black passengers are also getting off. Among them I notice a white man in shorts who is looking around. He walks up to me and shakes my hand. "Daan Taljaard," he says introducing himself. "Are you Hester van der Walt?" He loads my bags onto the back of a mud-spattered bakkie and stretches a tarpaulin over them. I haul myself up into the passenger seat beside him.

Nothing in my twenty-three years had prepared me for Venda in the 1960s. The gravel road between Louis Trichardt and Siloam wound through landscapes with clusters of thatched rondavels, unfamiliar trees and vegetation, and small patches of mealies and morog spinach cultivated in the red soil. Everything was strange, especially the people in the landscape. Women wearing only a piece of blue and grey striped cloth, knotted over one shoulder, some with bare breasts, the fabric tied at their hips. Babies were carried piggy-back and toddlers ran around naked. The women worked as hard as pack animals, carrying heavy loads on their heads – huge bundles of wood, or clay pots and tins filled with water. People waved and greeted us warmly. Barefoot school children ran alongside the road and every now and then we passed a simple school building or a shop with big Coca Cola or Omo adverts on the walls. On the stoep of every shop a man was sewing, bent over his sewing machine. After driving for over an hour, we reached a gate which spelled out our destination in separated letters on giant clay pots S I L O A M.

We drive up an avenue of tall flame trees which lead to a central square surrounded by low buildings, each with a covered stoep. The bottom half of all the walls are brown, the same shade as the soil. Women, men and children walk around dressed in blue hospital gowns. Most of the adults are painfully thin with sunken cheeks, and I notice many of the children have swollen faces and legs as thin as matchsticks. Kwashiorkor. Up till then I had only seen it in a text book. Acute malnutrition caused by lack of protein.

My eyes widen when Daan introduces me to Dr Evert Helms, his wife Dr Leida Helms, Dr Piet Scheele and Sister Dith Glasbergen. Instantly I feel drawn to Dith. She has dark-brown eyes and her thick, brown hair is pinned up and covered with a short veil. She glows with health and vitality and immediately makes me feel welcome. She takes me to the sisters' home which I will be sharing with Dith and Sister Van Welie. An ordinary house with a kitchen, bathroom, bedrooms and a communal sitting/dining room. Comfortably furnished. Sister Van Welie is the matron. A strict figure, reserved, probably in her late thirties. She tells me I will be in charge of the maternity division. "It is a pity that you are still waiting for your midwifery exam results, but a good thing you come here fresh from training." My heart beats wildly when I hear that more than one hundred babies are delivered here every month, and that I will also be responsible for the ante-natal clinics and the mothers and babies in the post-natal ward.

When I recall that time, I wonder how I could have accepted such immense responsibility. Could I have refused? Was I so eager to be of service? All the sisters and doctors were from the Netherlands. They were hard-working and dedicated. How could I not play my part? For emergencies, I could call the doctor on duty, but at night only one doctor was on call for the whole hospital and he needed to get some rest if at all possible. I remember reading my trusted little red Maggie Myles textbook deep into the night. The two staff nurses who had been in the ward for many years saved me. They taught me the routine and I lost no time in practising essential phrases in Tshivenda: "Take a deep breath. Don't push. Now, push! Yes, that's good. It's a boy! It's a girl!" The nurses could speak English, but the patients could not.

In the ante-natal clinic I gain first-hand experience of women's fashions in Venda. Row upon row of pregnant women sit waiting to be examined by the staff nurse and me. Some wait on the ground in the shade of the giant flame trees. They are barefoot. Their legs, from the ankle to just below the knee, are covered in bracelets of metal or wire. Our next patient, Musekwa, flings her striped shoulder cloth over her head, spreads it over the hospital draw sheet, and lies down on top of it, naked except for the small, square, striped apron covering her vulva. During my first months there I work with an interpreter to understand each woman's medical history. I take her blood pressure, palpate her abdomen with fingers becoming more practised at ascertaining foetal development and position. I make another discovery when it is time to examine her genitals. Musekwa pulls up her knees and the little apron flaps back. There is no broekie! The apron of double-folded cloth was neatly covering a groin-strap of beads. Musekwa gets up and smiles widely when she hears all is well. She throws the striped cloth back over her left shoulder and off she goes again: just as elegant, with jingling ankle bracelets.

Soon after my arrival in Siloam, I discovered there was another vacancy for a nursing sister. I wondered whether Lies might be interested. It would depend on how her mother was and whether Lies had already found work in Bloemfontein. I missed her and wrote to her often about Venda and my work in the hospital. And of course I mentioned all my Dutch colleagues. Years later I discovered Lies still kept one of those letters in her purse! My descriptions of Siloam were apparently so captivating that she could not resist applying for the position. A few weeks later she arrived for the interview, with her mother and Nico. She was still a bit unsure, but the die was cast and Lies was offered the post and also moved into the nursing sisters' house.

Many years later, I realised how naive my political consciousness was at this time. To some extent my decision to move to Venda was a protest against the apartheid I had witnessed in District

Six and Cape Town. I was blissfully unaware that Bantustans or the so-called homelands were really the basic building blocks of Verwoerd's apartheid policy. Gradually I began to piece together the bigger picture. Venda was one of ten separate areas proclaimed as a homeland for Tshivenda-speaking people in 1962. It was supposed to give people the opportunity to govern themselves and protect their culture, but in reality its purpose was to deprive black people of their rights to land and citizenship in South Africa. Most of the men worked on mines in the Witwatersrand and only came home once a year. Venda still fell under South African administration and all major decisions had to be approved by the administrator in Sibasa.

On Sunday mornings Dith liked to pack a basket with sandwiches and coffee into the boot of her Volkswagen, collect a few young schoolboys to act as interpreters, and drive into the mountains to give Sunday school classes at a remote school built of mud. Dith told a Bible story, illustrated with images on a felt board, which the school boys interpreted. Lies and I took turns accompanying Dith. We regularly attended the black Reformed Church services at Siloam, but were actually members of the white congregation in Louis Trichardt where we did not feel at all at home; yet every three months the elders arrived to find out if we were ready to receive communion.

It is dusk when the two brothers from the church, a deacon and an elder, knock at the door of the sisters' home. Dith opens the door and invites them inside. She telephones the wards and Lies and I arrive separately. Lies draws the curtains and we take our seats in the sitting room. Brother Venter, the elder, clears his throat nervously. "I hear you also always close the curtains when black men come to visit." We stare at him, surprised. What is he talking about? He continues. It has come to their attention that we are overly familiar with black people and that every Sunday we drive off into the veld with two young black men. "It has come to the attention of the church council, and we wish to warn you that you are playing with fire. In addition, you are endangering the mission's work." We are speechless with astonishment. We try to explain that the schoolboys interpret for us. The atmosphere is ice-cold when they leave.

We get into the Volkswagen, weeping with helpless rage, and drive into the veld to get away from a house that no longer feels like home, because someone is watching us.

....

We are visiting Oupa and Ouma in the Strand. I run under the fig trees all the way to Ouma's kitchen. The whole family is sitting on the stoep, drinking coffee. Everyone speaks at the same time. They laugh and wave their hands about. Nobody notices me standing near the steps. When I look around, he is standing there; Johan, my oldest cousin. He is very tall because he is already sixteen. I am only nine. He is so strong that he can pick all of us up at once when we are playing. Today he is only wearing a shirt. A long shirt that almost reaches his knees. Odd. Is that all he is wearing, I wonder? I stretch out my hand and carefully lift the shirt. Just to see. Suddenly everybody starts to laugh, everybody is looking at me. "And what are you doing, sissie?" my Oom Koos asks.

I am so embarrassed that I turn and run away. Johan laughs too. He will probably never play with me again.

My almost childlike concept of sin, fear of rejection and determination to do the right thing was always part of me.

....

Soon after Lies's arrival at Siloam, Sister Van Welie left and Lies replaced her as matron. Responsibility for the hospital, patients and staff weighed heavily on Lies's shoulders and night after night I listened to the worries she brought home. Supplies ordered but never delivered. Doctors who didn't understand how difficult it was for nurses (with very little formal education) to understand instructions delivered in broken English with strong Dutch accents. Nurses who were negligent and had to be reprimanded. On top of all this, we worked in isolation in a very small community and were mutually dependent on colleagues twenty-four hours a day. The highlight of the week was Bible study and Tshivenda lessons on a Thursday evening! It was important to get away for a few days regularly, in order to return with fresh courage and dedication. We took turns to go on leave. For my first break, Dith and I went to Mozambique for two weeks.

When it is Lies's turn for a break, the two of us go to Saint Lucia. We stay in a simple thatched rondavel on the beach, eat fish fresh from the sea every day and walk for miles along the sand. We feel as if the whole world belongs to us, there is not another soul in sight. We spread our towels beneath the pine trees when we need a rest. One perfect day glides into another. As the shadows lengthen, it gets cooler beneath the trees. One day I must have fallen asleep, and when I wake we are lying close together, side by side. I am intensely aware of the whole length of Lies's warm body against my cooler skin. A tingling I have suppressed for so long washes through me like a golden wave. Excitement. Bliss. Joy. All at the same time. I shift and turn over to face her. Her eyes are open and she looks straight at me. She smiles. I leap up, alarmed, fold my towel and pull my shirt over my swimming costume.

That night a tropical storm hits us. The rafters groan and we discover that the rondavel's windows don't close properly. After we put out the light, Lies creeps into bed with me. We hold each other tight all night. I stay awake, marvelling over this new intimacy in our friendship. Is it sinful? We discuss this often. We can't decide, but something this delicious probably is unrighteous! We have been friends for five years and trust each other. But being passionately in love is another matter. Can two women love one another? Are they allowed to? One thing is certain: no one must know about this and we solemnly promise each other that we will keep our newly discovered feelings secret.

In the weeks and months that follow, we discover how difficult it is to keep this secret. One day I accompany a young mother to theatre for her caesarean section. Lies is the theatre sister working alongside Dr Piet Scheele who is operating. Lies's eyes seem a particularly vivid blue today, glowing against her brown skin. They sparkle when she looks at me. We stand in the small operating theatre of Siloam. I feel the warm blood creep up my cheeks under the mask and I look away, alarmed. Is she mad? We are not alone here! Fortunately Piet, Dith and Sister Makonde bustle around the patient who is still under anaesthetic. The caesar is a great success. Lies assists Piet. She grips the needle expertly with tweezers while he closes the wound, first the layers of subcutaneous tissue and then finally the skin. I concentrate on the baby. She looks healthy and I give her an Apgar score of eight out of ten. Yet my focus is still on Lies. We will have to be careful. I feel the stirring of our love throughout my entire body. And the anxiety and shame. What are we going to do? Lies is far too reckless. Doesn't she realise it is extremely dangerous to look at me like that?

It is night. The dark night of reckoning. Lies and I are on our way back to Siloam where we have been working as nursing sisters for eight months. We can't hide from ourselves any longer; we are madly in love with each other. And all we know for certain is that this love is sinful.

Lies parks the pale yellow Cortina beside the Mauluma river, before we have to drive through the first shallow crossing; the gravel road criss-crosses the river four times. The car's windows are open and the tropical night envelops us in a symphony of sound. Frogs, crickets and in the distance the rhythmic beat of drums. A dense mopane forest where we have often picnicked lines one side of the road. It is high summer. We are both wearing the new miniskirt dresses we bought in Louis Trichardt that afternoon, hers has blue and white stripes and mine orange and white.

"We must decide now, before we cross this river. Either we stay together, or we separate and never see each other again," Lies says. "We can't go on like this any longer."

We have been weeping the whole way, since leaving the hotel where we spent the weekend. We begin circling through the options again; which one of us will leave and for where? Or do we leave together? Where would we go? I begin to sob again, crumpling the wet hanky between my fingers.

"But I love you! And how can love be a sin? Isn't Jesus supposed to be Love? And we aren't hurting anyone!"

Who said this? I suppose I did – I have always been more comfortable with skirting the truth than Lies.

"Then we stay together, right here! We will find a way. But we will have to be careful, because walls have ears and there is danger everywhere. We can't speak about this to anyone."

Joy and relief. For now. Thuthuzela. We drive through all four streams. Lies stops after the last crossing, and we hold each other tight.

That was 1967. We never did make any promises, but after fifty years we are still together. For Now. My greatest treasures are still too precious to talk about lightly. But those times of being afraid and hiding away are gone forever.

6

Travels

A sepia photograph from 1969. I sit on a huge suitcase, wearing a thick coat with a knitted scarf around my neck. I am half-asleep after a restless night on the train from Trieste to Amsterdam. My feet are frozen in these big boots. The commotion of people on the move surrounds me. A voice calling. Trains whistling. Traffic. The scarf protects my nose from the bitter cold. Finally, we have arrived in Holland! Dith comes to fetch us. We are so happy to see her again. She bundles us into her yellow Volkswagen Beetle. I am amazed at the landscape: The first windmills I see just outside Leiden. Rows of gabled houses in the reclaimed polder land. Farms that look small and toy-like. We drive on the right-hand side of the road around traffic circles. Everything is cramped. Everybody is on their way somewhere, it's a normal work day. We seem to be the only wanderers; for over a month we have travelled by ship and train.

It feels like an eternity since we left Bloemfontein in light summer clothes. We sailed to Europe on the Italian ship, *Africa*. I was seasick for the first few days and when that passed I suffered from asthma and eventually ended up in the ship's hospital where the Italian doctor could not understand a word I said. Fortunately asthma is an international language and eventually my chest did clear up. I even went ashore briefly at Las Palmas, on shaky legs. We also called in at the harbours of

Brindisi and Venice. Dream cities which I experienced as if in a haze. I was anxious. Would I survive? Was I strong enough? Was it a mistake to travel this far? I felt like a burden to Lies, who nursed and comforted me patiently.

Dith had a tiny flat in Alphen aan den Rijn, in the building where she worked as a community nurse. She made up beds for us in the basement. We carried our suitcases down to a dimly lit room that housed the building's air conditioner. Dith had made it cosy with a carpet, table lamps and even a bowl of tulips. A window, high up on the wall, had a view of the street outside if you stood on tippy-toes.

Our first evening in the basement room. Alone at last. Lies crawls into bed with me and we hold one another. We can still hear Dith's footsteps above our heads. Suddenly a loud bang on the staircase sends Lies shooting out of my bed and into hers. Secrecy is part of our lives. No one must know of our stolen time together. A furtive affair. Not because we are cheating on anybody, but because we do not want to shock anyone, or cause offence, or risk rejection or be ostracised. The fear is deeply rooted. In our hearts we have known for at least three years that our love is not wrong, but we are still too afraid to confide in anyone else.

Looking back, I realise there must have been groups in the Netherlands at that time where people like us would have felt at home, where we could have spoken openly about our relationship. What impressed me most was the open and honest way the Dutch people interacted with one another. It often shocked me. They spoke about everything, nothing was sacred. There were discussions about religion and politics on the radio and television. People dared to question accepted truths. Nothing appeared to be off-limits. Sometimes my jaw literally dropped. But love between women? I heard nothing about that. And, to be honest, if I had heard anything I would probably have run a mile!

At Dith's insistence we met Esau du Plessis, the chief organiser of the Boycott Outspan organisation. He was also active in the Anti-Apartheid Movement in the Netherlands. He received us in his home in Leiden. A brown man from Cape Town who, after being compelled to live in Europe for years, spoke Afrikaans with a Dutch accent. He was bitter and cynical about South African politics. I sensed he mistrusted us and was testing us. And how naïve I was then! He laughed out loud when he heard we went to work in Venda to get away from apartheid. "What? It is a Bantustan created by the white masters precisely to preserve apartheid!" I hung my head. "Ja, but I only discovered that after I got there. Not from books or newspapers, but from my own experience of people dying of tuberculosis. And children dying from gastroenteritis and kwashiorkor."

Life is like that game where dominoes are arranged upright in long rows and patterns. Each block close enough to fall against the one in front. Consciousness is the light tap that tips the first domino. It is as subtle as a fresh idea that topples old unquestioned assumptions. As soon as one block tilts and topples into its nearest neighbour, all the dominoes begin to fall, one after another. The dominoes of new ideas also line up neatly, until they too are tested by a fresh wave of consciousness.

I remember the despair I felt after my first conversations with Esau, I wore my white skin and Afrikaner heritage like a cloak of shame. His bitter words barely concealed his longing to go back home. I could return tomorrow; he had to wait for the political system to change. Only after the revolution. For the first time I began thinking about the possibility of a revolution. I learnt to sing freedom songs with a group in Holland. Spanish, Portuguese and isiXhosa songs too.

Another domino that toppled overseas was my Reformed Church religious beliefs. Lies and I joined a Dutch group for a quick tour of Israel that year. We visited all the usual tourist destinations such as Jerusalem, Jericho, the Dead Sea and Bethlehem. We often chatted to the two Catholic priests in our group. At one of the sites, where archaeologists had unearthed artefacts and ancient scripts, I made a comment about creation and the age of the earth. The two priests looked at me in disbelief. "Do you believe that literally? That the world was created in seven days?" I nodded and asked: "What do you believe?" "Have you ever heard of evolution?" After that I began reading furiously about evolution and all the debates surrounding it. I was losing another frame of reference. Dutch newspapers were filled with news about new theological thinking about faith. I read opinions that echoed my wavering belief in original sin. "Is death truly a punishment?" asked one theologian. What would happen if everybody continued to live forever? No, death is part of the life cycle. My hungry spirit devoured these new ideas and new worlds opened up for me.

After a year in Europe – learning about freedom of speech and daring to live life to the full – we flew back to Bloemfontein. Our plans were vague, but Lies felt she should live near her mother. We planned to rent a flat and study psychiatric nursing.

While we were searching for nursing courses in Bloemfontein, we stayed with Lies's mother in her spacious flat. Tante Corry had settled down well after leaving Edenburg. She was so happy to see her daughter again. Towards me she was very warm in a brusque sort of way. I attributed it to Dutch unsentimental matter-of-factness, but did wonder whether she would rather be alone with Lies. In just a few months Tante Corry had created a comfortable home. Red geraniums on the balcony outside and clusters of pink begonias creeping down from the bookshelf inside. The heavy art deco armchairs and sideboard and the table where we ate three meals a day. Lies often played the organ that belonged to her father. *Hou u my hande beide, met krag omvat. (Hold both my hands, surround me with strength.)* I remember the arguments between Lies and her mother. About politics, of course. It was

1970 and Vorster was in power. In the Netherlands we had spent nights in conversation with anti-apartheid thinkers and activists. Esau du Plessis from the Boycott Outspan movement filled us with ideas of freedom and brotherhood. In Bloemfontein we were surrounded by white neighbourhoods where domestic workers or "ousies" arrived by bus early in the morning and left late in the afternoon with a plastic bag from their madams. Everything that had seemed invisible before, had acquired a sinister new aspect. I felt powerless and frustrated during the conversations with Tante Corry. I knew there was little she, or even we, could do, but nevertheless I was determined not to keep quiet. However one has to choose the right time and place to deliver newly discovered truths. Tante Corry had enough challenges of her own to deal with. After a week or two of futile searching in Bloemfontein, we decided to look for training courses in Cape Town.

Lies stands in the passage in front of the hat stand, with the big grey telephone in her hand. She dials enquiries and finally gets the telephone number for the Red Cross Children's Hospital. We know it is in Rondebosch, but have only a vague idea of where that is. Lies dials the number, asks to speak to the matron and quickly hands the telephone to me. "They only speak English and she can't understand my accent."

The woman on the line introduces herself as Miss McMasters.

"Do you still have vacancies on your paediatric course for two nurses? ... Yes, we are qualified and we have completed midwifery."

She explains that the next course begins only in three months' time, but we can come and work in the hospital in the meantime to get familiar with the routines.

"When can we start?" I ask

"Immediately," she replies: "When can you get here?"

My heart gallops madly. "We will be there in three days," I

hear myself say. All she needs is our names, they are desperate for nursing staff, and yes, we can stay in the nurses' home.

With the help of her brother-in-law, Lies buys a second-hand Volkswagen Fastback in the space of one day. And off we go, heading for freedom, away from oppressive, suburban Bloemfontein.

7

A home in the Mother City

Did we drive straight through the night or did we break our journey somewhere? It was a tense trip. Lies was the only driver then and she was unfamiliar with her new car. Everything went smoothly, but driving on Cape Town's freeways was a huge challenge. I was holding the map and navigating – although I have no sense of direction and always struggle to tell left from right – and she began to panic. We asked for directions at a petrol station and finally pulled up in front of the Red Cross Children's Hospital's imposing modern building.

It is already five o'clock and Matron's office is closed. Someone takes us on a roundabout route to the nurses' home. We are each given a room on the sixth floor, at the end of a long, gloomy passage with doors on either side. The bathroom and toilets are in the middle of the passage. The hostel mother, a former nurse, still wearing her blue uniform, silk stockings and court shoes, gets us to sign in and gives us our keys and a list of rules: Visitors may only be received in the ground floor sitting room. No food in the rooms. Breakfast is at six o'clock in the dining room.

"And oh yes, before you go, remember pets are strictly forbidden."

I see her stare through the window vindictively. Outside in the garden a woman in uniform is walking a poodle on a lead. I realise this is a little female kingdom with its own petty feuds and victories.

The blue cotton bedspread is marked in the corner: CPA. Cape Provincial Administration. I fold it back across the foot of the single bed and crawl, bone-tired, between the starched white CPA sheets. As unfamiliar as a hospital bed. The South-Easter rattles the windows. I smell the sea air, breathe deeply and realise we are back in Cape Town. Knock-knock, knock-knock-knock from the wall above my head. Warmth, joy and recognition flood my body. I sit up and reply. Knock-knock, knock-knock-knock. A rapid staccato of knocks follows and I reply in code. It could mean anything, but in my heart I know she is saying: "It's strange, I know, but we will get through this too. I love you."

Cartwright Mansions on Greenmarket Square is one of those lovely old buildings. I have never been in such a tiny elevator cage. Fortunately a seated operator controls the copper knobs. Instead of a sliding door, a heavy iron gate clatters shut and we move jerkily upwards. I clutch my handbag with two months' rent tightly under my arm. I can see my profile in the big mirror. An old-fashioned girl in a sepia portrait. A serious, narrow face and dark eyes like the female ancestors in old photographs at my ma's home. On the third floor the gate is shifted open and I head down the passage looking for number 351, the estate agent's office. It's finally happening – our own home! I am excited but also afraid of making a mistake as Lies is on duty today and I have to conclude the transaction single-handedly.

The agent is a short man in his fifties. Red face and a neck that bulges over his tie. In my best English I explain that I have come to sign for the flat in Campground Road, Rondebosch. The one that was advertised in this morning's *Cape Times*.

"No Miss. That one's gone already," he replies casually. My world falls apart. This is too much for me to bear. The prospect of finally having a place of our own and getting away from the hostel where there is no privacy. After so much freedom in Holland, the nurses' home feels like a prison. To my horror my lower lip starts quivering and I burst into tears in front of this total stranger. He is taken aback. Apologises, offers his handkerchief.

"I'm so sorry my girl, but there was someone before you." Awkwardly he moves papers around his cluttered desk. I want to apologise for my behaviour and find a soggy tissue in my bag. He looks at me again. "Wait a minute, I have something else in that area." He gives me an address in Rosebank. Liesbeeck Road West. Bingo! I know Liesbeeck is near the hospital because we always drive past it. "Go and have a look. It has just come onto my list." I feel like hugging the man.

And so 10 Trelawney becomes our first real home. Lies teases me and tells everybody that we got the flat because I cried. The three-storey block is straight from the fifties, solid concrete and steel. The elderly Jewish lady in number 12 pokes her head out the door and stares through the safety gate to make sure we aren't undesirables. She mutters under her breath. I greet her warmly, only too grateful to be here and not in the nurses' home. Our two-roomed flat is on the second floor of the smallish block. Within walking distance of the Red Cross Children's Hospital, via the Rondebosch common. We have very little money, but we are creative and make every cent count. We find pine beds, a dining room table and four chairs in Salt River. We have foam rubber cushions and matresses cut to size in Woodstock. We buy a set of dark brown crockery and some cutlery at OK Bazaars. Throwing a tablecloth over our very own table for the first time on a Sunday morning and sitting down to a traditional Hoogendoorn family breakfast feels so momentous that it becomes a ritual: the essence of simplicity; boiled eggs, whole-wheat bread, cheese and jam and a cup of tea.

Today we are expecting our first guests and we are fully prepared. Our only comfortable furniture, two beds, are pushed lengthwise against the sitting room walls to serve as seating. Covered with woven bedspreads and a couple of colourful cushions they look fairly decent. Cups and saucers and tea paraphernalia are laid out on the table. At church last Sunday, Elder Venter introduced himself to the newcomers in his parish and made an appointment to visit us. "Naturally the visit is necessary in view of the upcoming holy communion service. I will bring Brother Duvenhage, our parish deacon, with me."

Lies opens the door and leads the two men inside, along the narrow passage. Brother Venter formally introduces us to Brother Duvenhage: "This is Sister Van der Walt and Sister Hoogendoorn."

"Just call me Lies."

Brother Venter sees the beds and quickly looks around the room. "Don't you have a lounge?" he asks surprised. I have to hide my smile while Lies explains that we are also using our beds as sofas for the time being. Is this man afraid we are going to seduce them? They seat themselves on the chairs at the dining room table. Brother Venter notices the cups and quickly says: "Unfortunately we don't have time for tea today, Sister. We have many people to visit before it gets too late."

The elder reads a few Bible verses about loving one's neighbour. Then he wants to know whether we feel eligible to receive communion, that is to say, have we perhaps committed any sins against a fellow brother or sister that might prevent this? He looks very relieved when we assure him we have nothing to confess. For a moment there is silence in the room. From the flat above ours a mother calls to her children who are playing on the tarmac outside. The summer evening's last rays of light stream through the window. Brother Venter shifts around. His heavy body is uncomfortable on the hard pine chair.

"One more thing. We noticed that you do not wear hats to church. Women must wear hats in our church. It is part of our tradition." He looks inquiringly at Lies and me.

We stay silent. The clock strikes seven. His face turns red and he clears his throat. I choose my words with care.

"I wonder why people are so intolerant towards those who do things differently?" I take a deep breath before I continue. "Is it also tradition that only white people attend our church? How would you feel if I brought my brown friends to church? Would they be welcome?"

A fish seller's horn breaks the silence and all four of us turn to look outside. As if we welcome the distraction.

Then Brother Venter notices the large print on the wall beside him. Tretchikoff's two black pennywhistle players. He looks away quickly, disapprovingly. He stows his Bible in his briefcase and says vehemently: "No, look here, you are taking things much too far. The Word does indeed say that you should love your neighbour like yourself, but that implies that you must love yourself first. What you two want to do will lead to self-destruction!"

Lies and I look at each other, say nothing. Lies shrugs. Outside the children laugh and play. The man gets up and shuts his briefcase decisively. We lead the way out, towards the closed front door. We turn to face them and we all shake hands. Formally.

The next moment there is a knock on the door. The two startled men step aside while our colleague Bee Lubelwane bursts in, laughing, and embraces me warmly.

And that was more or less the beginning of the end of our association with the Reformed Church. No, the church did not suspend us; we gave up our membership.

During the early seventies we became involved with Beyers Naudé's Christian Institute which had offices in Mowbray, near the station. I remember the lively debates about what it meant to be a Christian in our country. The flamboyant brown Anglican priest Clive McBride was a beacon of light. He was fascinated by us, two white Afrikaans girls in search of truth and justice and convinced that apartheid was wrong. I remember long conversations with him in his sitting room in Factreton, a poor neighbourhood near Maitland. He was on a one-man mission to touch hearts and open minds. On Mondays, his day off, he would pack a basket of sandwiches and coffee and drive to Stellenbosch with the intention of giving lifts to hitch-hiking students and engaging them in conversation. I imagine they readily accepted a lift from such a well-spoken, charming man. If the only brown people you have known all your life were subservient servants, Clive would certainly be a revelation! And as the conversation progressed, he might stop and offer coffee from his flask and a sandwich, and gently introduce the politics of the day. They would exchange telephone numbers and arrange to bring a group of student friends to continue the discussion and visit his congregation in Factreton.

Clive encouraged us to remain within our church and act like yeast. But it didn't work out. The last straw was a house visit from the dominee himself. He was clearly perplexed by the two rebellious sisters who refused to stop questioning things.

"Look here," the dominee finally said, exasperated, "if you want to marry black men, move to Swaziland. That kind of thing is permitted there!"

We stared at him, stunned, and tried to explain that we were not motivated by marriage. Shortly afterwards I wrote a letter to the church council formally resigning as a member of the church. Lies did the same. Neither of us received a reply. Even members of the congregation who had been friendly towards us broke off all contact and did not even greet us in the street. I think they were all too relieved that we had left.

The Christian Institute in Mowbray was a hive of activity. The old house had been divided into a warren of spaces. The Black Sash Advice Office occupied one room, counselling black people who were involved in a life and death struggle with the Bantu Administration for the right to live and work in Cape Town. Theo Kotze was the head of the Christian Institute and we got to know him and his wife at meetings held regularly in the library. We met a wonderful cross-section of people there. Quakers like June Humphrey and Catholics (ja, that *Roomse Gevaar*, or Roman Catholic threat, we were always warned about as children). In particular, I remember Barbara Versveld, her husband Marthinus, a much-loved author and philosopher, and their large family. Students from the universities of Cape Town and the Western Cape also came to this house of light during that dark depressing time of political impotence. Discussions always hinged on what we could do to be part of the solution, how we could help spread information to raise consciousness. We felt especially drawn to the Moravians – young and open-minded, brown and Afrikaans speaking. Robbie Krige and Frits Faro invited us to their Saturday discussions at the Moravian Church seminary in District Six. District Six? Were people still living there? I had been so saddened and shocked to see the bald patches on the slopes of Table Mountain where, ten years previously, I had witnessed so much love and sorrow during my midwifery training.

We drive up Constitution Street. Here is a mosque, still standing, surrounded by wild fynbos. The tarred road is full of potholes and the South-Easter blows litter around all over the place. The only buildings the state has not demolished are the churches. Lies parks in front of the Moravian Church, a lovely old Victorian building. Next door, in an overgrown garden with tall palm trees, is the Moravian Seminary where students are trained. We know Wolfgang Schäfer from the Christian Institute and he hugs us warmly. A German who is well-versed in Cape Afrikaans, thanks to his students. His blue eyes blaze as he gets fired up about the subject of the day: liberation theology in South America, North America and now here, in

South Africa. The Saturday discussions are open to anyone who is interested and wants to use these ideas to make sense of our everyday lives. The discussion is lively and informal. Articles are copied on a huge old photostatting machine that frequently breaks down. I learn about liberal European thinkers such as Bultmann and gain a fresh understanding of Jesus and the meaning of his life for the downtrodden people of today. Camaraderie grows over mugs of instant coffee, thick slices of bread and apricot jam. The atmosphere is jovial. I watch Lies's eyes glow. We have come home. To a spiritual home outside the church.

In 1976 the state cracks down on all organisations and activists still daring to protest against apartheid. The Christian Institute is banned and Beyers Naudé is placed under house arrest. Many people are detained without trial and tortured. During that time I realise that darkness has many shades and can become darker still. Steve Biko is already a well-known name, but a few of our Moravian friends become more active in the Black Consciousness movement and, overnight, begin to avoid us. Today I understand that it was a natural and necessary outlet for their fury, but back then I experienced it as yet another painful rejection.

....

Lies drives the Volkswagen Fastback. Edith, her so-called co-driver who cannot drive, sits beside her. Sally and I are in the back, with the cooler box, sleeping bags and pillows between us. Our new tent and four suitcases are on the roof-rack. The January sun casts long shadows across the Karoo koppies. "Look, there is the first of the Three Sisters," I tell our passengers who have never driven this road before. We left Cape Town early in the morning after stopping at Elsie's River to collect Sally and Edith. We cannot drive faster than 80 kilometres per hour because of fuel restrictions introduced after the oil embargo against South Africa. We all fall silent after a day of high spirits. It is getting late and we have to find somewhere to camp for the night; our first night ever in a tent.

"It's probably best to just pull off and sleep beside the road," Edith suggests hesitantly. Her fingers carefully stroke her long hair, a habit when she is feeling nervous. We pass a farm fence with a signboard: *Accommodation. One Kilometre.* Lies slows down. "Let's just go and find out," I say, more bravely than I feel. We turn in at the gate. The farm track makes a slow curve. There is a copse of poplars and willow trees beside a pretty dam. Green grass. An ideal place to camp. Lies and I walk to the homestead, and two tail-wagging ridgebacks come to meet us, followed by a man and woman in their forties. The woman unties her apron while I ask if we can camp beside the dam for the night.

"But why do you want to camp?" she asks, surprised. "We have comfortable rooms in the house and you are more than welcome." I stand my ground: "No thank you, we'd rather camp near the dam and we have everything we need." "All right then, do as you wish," the man says with a smile.

We almost skip back. Sally and Edith have already removed the tent from the roof-racks. Sally chops an onion and fries it with tomatoes on our new gas stove. After the drone of the highway all day, we appreciate our peaceful green campsite. It's a struggle to set up the tent, but Edith finally, with satisfaction, hammers in the last tent pegs. Fortunately the ground is damp near the dam. Lies is busy shaking out the sleeping bags when we hear voices. Mr and Mrs Botha. "I see you are settled in. If you want fresh water, feel free to get some from the kitchen." They leave. We look at each other. We say nothing but feel grateful. "You see, everything is fine," Lies says. Sally's smoortjie smells delicious and I slice the bread.

Just as we begin eating the Bothas return, this time accompanied by an adolescent son and daughter. They look different.

Red in the face. "How dare you bring Hotnots to come and sleep on my land! You have five minutes to pack up and go."

A turtle dove coos. I'm so scared, I can't say a word. They turn around and walk off. The children look back and laugh. Tears stream down my cheeks, but there is no time to cry. We quickly throw everything back into the car. How did we manage to fit it all in this morning? Sally comforts me against her short, firm body. "Ag never mind, don't cry like that. We are used to it!" Edith agrees with everything Sally says, but I can see how she is shaking. As we leave Mr Botha closes the gate behind us. His face is tight as he comes closer. "A Greek lives about twenty kilometres further on. Perhaps he will give you somewhere to camp."

When it grows dark Lies pulls off at a picnic site beside the highway. We make ourselves as comfortable as possible for a night in the car. A crescent moon hangs high above the Three Sisters and the four sisters.

We drive to Bloemfontein the next day. The idea was to spend the weekend with Lies's mother, Tante Corry. I don't feel as brave as yesterday. Anything can happen. Were we rash to think we could go on holiday together? But Sally and Edith had told us they had never been further than Bainskloof near Wellington. All holiday resorts, hotels and even camp sites had the hateful "Whites only" signs. It seemed natural to invite them along on our trip to Siloam in Venda. The four of us were colleagues at Red Cross Children's Hospital and had all completed the course in paediatric nursing. The same one-year diploma but in different classes. Each lecturer had to deliver the same lecture twice, to two small groups of not more than twelve students. One group white, the other brown. The practical training, however, was in the hospital where all the students worked with the same children. It was in one of the wards that I first met Sally. A few years older than me, short, a bit plump, with a sunny disposition. She had far more experience than me and taught me how to soak bandages before removing them from the little body of a child who had been badly burnt, while all the time chatting calmly to young Roedewaan. She was the motherly type, feet firmly on the ground. She knew about hardships, I discovered when I met her large family in their run-down home in Elsie's River amidst large factories and barbed wire fences. Her salary had to pay for the family's food and school fees. Edith Nelson was different. In spite of her English name, she was an Eastern beauty. Long black hair, enormous eyes and a slender figure. She was more introverted and very private. We offered to collect her from her home, but as usual she preferred to meet us at Sally's home with her luggage. They knew each other well and had worked together for many years in the children's ward of Conradie Hospital.

At five o'clock we arrive at Tante Corry's first floor flat in suburban Bloemfontein. She receives us warmly and succeeds in hiding any possible surprise about the colour of our friends. Twenty minutes later Lies's sister Corry arrives. She and her young family live just two blocks away. She brings extra mattresses for our friends and is of course eager to see Lies. After Lies's sister leaves, we make up the beds on the floor and Tante Corry warms up her famous tomato soup with meat balls. She goes to answer the phone in the passage, and asks me to watch the soup. I sense her tension when she calls Lies to the telephone. The voices are soft but gradually Lies's voice becomes more vehement and I go closer. Lies's sister has called to warn their mother that she could get into serious trouble if her neighbours report that she has accommodated non-whites. Now Tante Corry is scared and unsure. What if the police arrive and evict her from her flat? Lies is furious with her sister. What do we do now? The Three Sisters debacle of yesterday evening replays in my head. Sally and Edith are quiet and insecure. A hotel is out of the question. There are many expensive hotels in the big cities which accommodate black and brown visiting statesmen, but nothing in Bloemfontein. It is Saturday and we cannot drive much further this weekend with a quarter tank of petrol. By now Tante Corry is in tears. She wrings her hands together. She is so used to receiving everybody warmly, and she is at a loss. Then she says firmly: "Whatever happens, people need three good meals a day. You cannot drive any further now, so you will stay here tonight." We take our places at her oak table with its solid round feet and she spoons warm red soup into her beautiful deep bowls. We close our eyes for the usual silent grace at mealtimes. Sally fills the silence: "Father, bless this meal, may we never forget you."

During the meal I make a decision. Welkom, where my parents live, was never part of our holiday route, but, I am going to call my ma and ask if we can spend the weekend there. It is not an easy decision. Ma and I have avoided all discussion of politics since she told me our government knew what it was doing. I knew she still voted for the National Party.

She is surprised to hear my voice. "Hester, is that you? What a surprise!" We do not phone each other regularly, even though I try to write as often as possible. Then, with a mother's intuition, she asks tentatively: "Is everything all right?" Her voice is full of concern and stirs the young child within me. To my dismay my lower lip quivers so much I can hardly speak. Then the words tumble out. "Ma, we are in Bloemfontein, but we would like to come to Welkom tomorrow." "But of course, my child! Stefaans is on night shift so you can have his room."

I hesitate. I know all old certainties have become uncertain. Even the everyday act of using a public lavatory at a petrol station is no longer normal. Your friends are turned away and you are not. Only now I know what it feels like to be unwelcome, to be chased away. I sob quietly. Openly. I who do everything I can to hide my true feelings from Ma. I manage to speak: "Ma, please listen. We have two friends with us.

We all work together at the hospital. They are … brown … coloured …" I say the hated word. I realise now that people should rather spell things out clearly. There is silence at the other end of the line.

Then, after what feels like an eternity, she says: "Hester, you know what your brother Hendrik always tells me – ag Ma, don't worry about what other people think or say about you, forget about them. We will work it out my child. By all means, come." I sob loudly. From gratitude. Warmth. Pride. All mixed up together. "We have a tent, Ma. We can pitch it in the backyard."

And so we spend the rest of the weekend at my parents' rented house. A mining house, 9 Mitchell Street. Ma stands on the stoep waiting for us, with my sister Anetha, a teenager of fifteen. She hugs me tightly and whispers: "Pa says you are not to stay in a tent; we won't allow that!"

The initial awkwardness changes within minutes to an easy banter. Sally and Edith are Capetonians after all and my ma immediately feels at home with them. Within half an hour Sally and Anetha are discussing make-up, and Sally even plucks a few unruly hairs from Anetha's eyebrows. It is cosy and congenial. Ricoffy and Ma's little meat pies. I feel a load fall from my shoulders. Never again will I be ashamed of my family. I always thought the Dutch were so politically enlightened and my family was backwards, but I know now that there is a difference between word and deed.

When I look back at that time, now that our country has a constitution which protects human rights, I am struck by how we were all contaminated by the tyranny of those times. Everybody was terrified of putting a foot wrong, in case they contravened some law or another. Nobody could trust anyone else or be spontaneous. Lies's sister, an immigrant, had felt threatened herself, and so had the farming folk of Three Sisters. As soon as you deprive one person of his rights to citizenship, you deprive everyone.

… mag daar altyd mense wees
wat mekaar sonder skaamte in
die oë kan kyk –
want die lewe is 'n asem lank
en die sterre op die Anderplek donker –

— Breyten Breytenbach

… may there always be people
who can look each other in
the eye without shame –
because life is as long as a breath
and the stars in the Other Place are dark –

In 1976 when the first trails of tear gas start to swirl through the streets of Cape Town, number 10 Trelawney becomes a temporary refuge for friends who dare not stay at their own homes. There is always a place to sleep for everybody. The neighbours are uneasy with this open house policy and one morning two policemen knock on our door. "We hear you have some trouble here." I put on my friendliest smile. "It must be a false alarm, Sir. All is well here." In the adjacent bedroom, Nthambeleni packs his suitcase. He knows it is time to leave Cape Town.

8

The Flats

The surgical dressing station I prepared so carefully early this morning – neat stacks of sterile bandages, clean linen on the beds – looks more and more like a war zone. The rubbish bins are filled with gauze bandages and sweet wrappers. Even the sharp smell of disinfectant from Savlon and the soap dispensers at the basins cannot mask the scent of poverty; old sweat and unwashed socks, jerseys and jackets that smell of mould and cigarette smoke. The last patient vomited on the floor and workers are mopping up the mess: "Couldn't the mother have taken the child to the toilet?"

It's Monday, always a busy day at Heideveld Day Hospital. The corridors are packed with row upon row of people waiting to see the doctors or nurses. Children play. Women exchange news and advice but everyone listens for the sound of feet, the great moment when your name is finally called. The clerk comes down the corridor with a pile of green folders in one hand. She calls shrilly: "Gadidja Abrahams, I repeat, Gadidja A-bra-hams! Johannes Barends, Johannes Barends! Sarah September! Samuel van Wyk!" Samuel is a small boy. The left side of his head is shaved and his large, dark eyes look around the dressing station fearfully. His file, I see, states that he is thirteen. He clutches the clumsy bandage around his right arm anxiously. It looks like a nappy. I give him a chair and talk softly to gain his trust. "What happened, Samuel?" "I got stabbed, Nurse," he tells me once

I have removed the covering and can examine the superficial wound in the fleshy part of his upper arm. I rinse the wound carefully with weak saline solution. It stings, and his eyes fill with tears. He swallows and wipes the tears away with the back of his undamaged hand. His grey school trousers and polished shoes are neat. He is just a child, I suddenly realise and I ask him about school. He begins to relax just a bit and then my colleague spots him.

"Ja, you!" she says sharply. "It's because you are all so bloody naughty that these things happen! Where were you roaming around this weekend? You're supposed to be in school today, and instead you come here to waste our time. If you carry on like this you will also become a gangster!"

Samuel winces and crumples up like someone who is used to dodging blows aimed at him. The more she rants, the softer I speak to Samuel. I want to hold him against me to shield him from her outburst but once again I feel overwhelmed by impotence.

How did I end up in that dressing station? If I think back to that time, I can see I chose jobs I hoped would make a difference to the lives of people who were suffering. Awakening one's consciousness is a long and gradual process, and I understand now that my choices led to a series of insights. After several years at Red Cross Children's Hospital I realised that the burnt and dehydrated children we treated constantly returned to the hospital with the same preventable "illnesses". I resigned from my job in 1974 and enrolled for a one-year diploma in Community Health at Cape Town Technikon, which I paid for. I led a student's life, catching the train to the city every day, walking across the colourful Grand Parade, past the grand old City Hall to the classroom, where I unexpectedly discovered a soul mate. Jootje Monnik was my lecturer. She came from the Netherlands and worked for the World Health Organisation in India and Indonesia for many years. She was a free spirit, way ahead of her time and a breath of fresh air in the often bigoted ranks of higher education in nursing. Under her guidance I embarked on creative research and became enthusiastic about the prospect of working within the community.

I began working at the Day Hospitals in 1975. The organisation, which fell under the Cape Provincial Administration, included seventeen hospitals spread across the whole peninsula. Its goal was to supply accessible primary health care close to the homes and workplaces of low income communities.

Perhaps at this point I should say something about my relationship with my nursing colleagues. From the outset, during my first few months as a student nurse, I realised that I had to find a way to fit in if I was to survive in nursing. I was different; softer, more sensitive, or, as I now believe, maybe more in touch with the basic soft-heartedness we are all born with. Being different was not necessarily a good thing! Certainly not in a profession where nurses were under pressure to pack more and more work into an eight- or twelve-hour shift. No wonder that young, idealistic women are quickly socialised by their senior colleagues into *feeling* less and *doing* more, faster! Early in the twentieth century, the nursing workload was divided into specific tasks – in a manageable, but deadly dull routine which instructed the nurse to care for the patient according to compartmentalised duties. For example, in one ward a single nurse had to give all thirty patients their injections – or wound care – between nine and ten o'clock in the morning. (This system is the opposite of holistic care, where one nurse is responsible for the comprehensive care of five or six patients.) The task-orientated approach dates back to the industrial revolution, the so-called conveyer belt approach, and unconsciously contributed to the carer becoming emotionally dulled and less involved with the person to whom the wound belonged.

The Day Hospitals were potentially places of healing and education. They were situated in the patients' neighbourhoods, and on their way to work every day staff could see the over-crowded blocks of flats, each one marked by gang graffiti and laden washing lines. They could see the children playing in the streets and the unemployed men standing and smoking on every corner. How could doctors, nurses, clerks and even cleaners frequently act so coldly and apparently heartlessly towards the people seeking their help? All I could do was show my softer side and hope it would make a difference. Colleagues reacted differently to my approach; some acted even more roughly with patients, and some just walked off. They also gossiped about me. I remember one incident early in my career when I visited a patient in the ward during my time off, just to see how she was doing and to raise her spirits. The sister on duty called me over and made it clear I was not welcome, as she did not want nurses to become "too involved" with their patients.

In spite of the "these people are born this way and there is nothing you can do" attitude expressed by most of our colleagues, just before Christmas, during a quiet period, Virginia Meyer and I started playing with a few bored children who were hanging around in the hospital garden. This gave us the idea to start a health club and the Sunshine Club was born. We handed out toothbrushes and sang songs to teach the children playful ways of brushing correctly. When a scabies epidemic hit the area and schools, we were invited to talk to teachers and school children. We wrote new lyrics for a popular song, *Hey Fatty Boom Boom*, and everyone sang along.

> *Hey naughty scabies, we are not afraid*
> *Hey naughty scabies, you cannot catch us*
> *We itch and we scratch and we waited too long*
> *The sores get bigger and bigger*

Then the refrain:

> *We wash with soap and water every day*
> *Hang blankets outside on a sunny day*
> *The Day Hospital has medication*

Soon we had an entire repertoire of songs, as well as board games, about tooth decay and protein-rich foods. I discovered jewels in the dust. Some were rough diamonds, like Nancy Geach, the Day Hospital's English-speaking head matron. A down-to-earth woman who never looked dignified in her tight uniform of navy-blue crimplene. She had none of the stiff formality of a typical matron. She encouraged Virginia and me to spend a few hours every day on "health education" – to the consternation and envy of some colleagues who definitely didn't view this as "work". We created all kinds of clubs; one for the many people with high blood pressure and another for diabetic patients, as well as a network devoted to malnourished children and their mothers. The patients enjoyed the personal attention and all children like to play. We began producing our own information leaflets. The official pamphlets and posters at this time were written in inaccessible language and were boring and colourless.

I went home to Lies with many stories about my work's new direction and she helped me design material. She was still working in the operating theatre at Red Cross Children's Hospital, and it was taking its toll on her. The only patients she saw were under anaesthetic, and she longed for something more fulfilling. When Virginia took study leave, Lies joined me in the Health Education Unit. It was the beginning of a period of creative collaboration. We started a puppet theatre and Abie Scabie quickly became one of our most popular characters. Dr John Smith, the superintendent, was our greatest supporter and he suggested we visit all seventeen Day Hospitals to train staff in counselling skills. This created a dilemma, because actually every contact between a patient and member of staff is an opportunity to listen and give the appropriate counselling. Busy waiting rooms where anxious people awaited their turn were hardly suitable places for didactic lectures. And so we began running workshops where staff could exchange ideas about how to communicate with patients effectively. These group sessions were called Communication Workshops and provided a space where colleagues could express their frustrations and support one other. We began the sessions by talking about the social and economic causes of the prevalent illnesses we dealt with at the hospitals, about the poverty around us and our relationships with the patients. We were strongly influenced by the work of Brazilian educator Paulo Freire. He used visual stimuli as codes to make people look at everyday realities with new eyes. Slowly, very slowly, we began to gain our colleagues' trust and inspire them about what they could do. After a few years we had a network of sisters in every centre. We supplied them with teaching material and visited them regularly.

....

Mrs Samuels has her hands full. Her right arm holds her nine-month-old baby, her left hand pulls along her daughter who I guess is two years old. A slight child. All eyes and tight plaits. Mrs Samuels also manages to carry a plastic bag containing things she needs for a day's outing to Heideveld Day Hospital. Doctor Daya has referred them to us for counselling and advice at the Nutrition Clinic. I draw up two chairs and clear a space at the table where Lies has been covering a poster with plastic. Lies will conduct the interview with Mrs Samuels. We have an arrangement to take turns. While the one is counselling, the other quietly carries on with her tasks in the adjoining room, but listens to the conversation so we can give each other feedback. From Lies's interview I discover that little Evelyn is already four years old. Her condition is known as "stunted growth", indicative of serious chronic malnutrition. It is far from unusual as roughly one third of the children in this area are underweight for their age. Up to the age of eighteen months their development is monitored by clinic sisters, but as soon as they have received all their vaccinations they simply fall through the cracks and become chronically underweight and susceptible to every illness. Mrs Samuels promises to attend the Nutrition Clinic the following week.

The following Tuesday afternoon, Mrs Samuels arrives at the Nutrition Clinic with her baby and little Evelyn. Each child's weight is monitored, but the main purpose is to give the mothers light-hearted, uncritical support and to encourage them to give each other advice about feeding their families. We supply enriched milk powder to add to their daily porridge. And we teach the children an action song about protein.

Let us sing now about the food that makes us grow,
From plants there are four that you know.
There are peas, peas
There are beans, beans
There are lentils and peanuts.

Let us sing now about the food that makes us grow
From animals there are four that you know
There are eggs, eggs
There is milk, milk
There is fish, fish
There is meat ja ja.

The little ones count every protein-rich food on their fingers and the mothers look proudly on as their clever children sing so enthusiastically. In this way the mothers learn too, without being lectured to or criticised. When we unpack the hand puppets there is great excitement. People have seen puppets on television but had no idea people could bring them to life and make them talk.

....

Lies and I discovered that we worked exceptionally well together as a team. We often worked with groups and afterwards would give each other feedback. Honest, candid feedback. "When you said we could move on to the next point, you were too quick, because shy Gladys had just scraped together all her courage and was about to say something!" Lies took photographs and together we developed texts for audio-visual programmes for counselling patients. We replaced the Department of Health's formal and inappropriate material with colourful posters and pamphlets designed to convey messages in people's own colourful colloquial Afrikaans.

In the late 1970s the nursing sisters asked us to work with the clerks who admitted patients to the hospitals. Admissions were always a place of conflict. Prospective patients must supply information about their income and make a contribution towards the minimum fee. Then their files must be tracked down, or a new file opened, and people were assigned to rows to wait, often for many hours. If the patient quota for the number of available doctors was filled for the day, and the ailment not too serious, people were asked to return the following day. During our workshops with the clerks it became clear that they worked under immense pressure. They reported directly to the hospital administrator and not to the matron or medical superintendent. In all health care services there is traditionally conflict over leadership and control between the administration and the heads of the medical and nursing departments. At the end of the workshop we proposed that the clerical staff compile a list of problems as well as their suggestions for improvements.

We attached the clerks' document to our report on the workshop and sent it to Dr John Smith and the administrator.

Two days later the axe fell. A telephone call from head office. Cancel all workshops with clerical staff. During the same week Dr John Smith and Matron Nancy Geach were removed, "transferred" away from the Day Hospitals. Dr Smith to the Conradie Hospital and Miss Geach to Groote Schuur. Broederbond? Who will ever know?

The following week Lies and I were called in by the new matron and ordered to discontinue all communication workshops until further notice. It was never spelt out in so many words, but I understood that we were being watched for any signs that we were "inciting the staff". It was the end of an era when we were free to determine the focus of our work ourselves. That space was always vulnerable, it floated like a balloon just above a wall topped with iron spikes. Every tiny glimpse of freedom was so rare and precious back then when the state's tentacles reached everywhere in the form of informers and eavesdroppers.

While working at the Day Hospitals I became a part-time student at the University of Cape Town. Late one afternoon, after work, I drive past our home in Observatory and take the turn-off to UCT. My heart pounds with anticipation. I had attended lectures at the UCT Summer School, but now I have enrolled for a Higher Diploma in Adult Education. At long last I am a university student! What will it be like? Will I be able to keep up or will the standard be too high? My mind churns as I drive up to the lofty portals of learning, on the slopes of Table Mountain. The old buildings are partly covered in creepers. Is this what they mean by Ivy League? Steep steps and imposing columns. Gorgeous young students, in spite of their faded jeans and careful attempts to appear as slovenly as possible. In the lecture hall Professor Clive Millar and Tony Morphet are waiting, along with Tony Saddington who I know from the Christian Institute and his involvement with our Day Hospital group workshops. Clive Millar informs us that it is the first Diploma in Adult Education at UCT and that our group of twenty are about to make history. The students are a diverse bunch, who are all actively involved in training and development work, mostly at non-governmental organisations such as Early Learning Research Unit, Grassroots Education Trust and trade unions. I am the only nurse but I feel at home from the start. Some people are older than me and everyone seems a little nervous about the academic side of the course, but we are all looking forward to the challenge.

These Monday and Thursday evening lectures become beacons along the path to a new adventure. I gulp down the theory hungrily and make it my own. I get corroboration for insights I arrived at through practical experience. Regardless of my initial insecurity, I enjoy the assignments and receive positive feedback about my work. It is so true; we are not empty vessels, we are already full of our own often untested theories! We work in small groups and get to know one another. Everyone's pet theories are listened to with the necessary respect and then unraveled and challenged. Not easy, but always interesting. Discussions centre inevitably on the politics of the day and we openly debate the restrictions on freedom of speech.

There is one Monday I will never forget. Clive Millar is clearly upset. "One of our students, Marian Jacobs, has left the course. She is convinced that there's an informer in our midst." He hands the podium to Tony Morphet. No names are mentioned. It isn't necessary. Everyone is a possible suspect. My illusion of finally being on a free campus also shatters. The "spy", most of us suspected, was an English-speaking white man who hardly said a word in class discussions, and subsequently left the class for "personal reasons". Was it him? Who knows?

9

Beyond hospital walls

In the early 1980s, in spite of the state's intimidation, banning and imprisonment of activists, people still became actively involved in new organisations like the United Democratic Front and all kinds of non-governmental organisations sprang up like toadstools. Johnny Issel, whom we had met at the Christian Institute and Moravian Hill, was a key figure. He invited us to talk about health matters at the Food and Canning Workers' Union's annual meeting in Paarl. He also drew us into *Grassroots*, a radical community newspaper that had been a weekly breath of fresh air in the townships since 1980. It carried news about issues affecting ordinary people and made them aware of the need for political change. This type of news and opinion never appeared in the commercial newspapers. Johnny asked Lies and I to join the *Grassroots*'s Advice Page Committee and give advice about health problems. The committee included a lawyer, a housing expert and a social worker. We met once a week to plan and edit the next edition's Advice Page.

This week the Advice Page Committee is meeting at our house in Oxford Street, Observatory. People start arriving around five thirty. Zubeida Jaffer is first. She is one of the full-time journalists at *Grassroots*. She drinks her mug of tea thirstily. "Today was rough. We were at Crossroads from very early this morning. People, there is serious trouble on the way with the Witdoeke."

Trevor Manuel explains how the Security Police (he calls them the Boere) are working with the Witdoeke to plan an attack on the Crossroads squatter camp. Lies and I pass around mugs of tea and coffee. Mr Chairman is late, as usual. When he does arrive, he is dressed to the nines. Black suit, white shirt and gleaming shoes. He was in court all day, he tells us.

Zubeida says we have a double-page spread in the next edition of *Grassroots*. Nobody has written in so far asking for our advice, and the column consists of questions and answers. But this is not a problem, Zubeida continues, the committee members have a good idea of what the issues are out there, so: write a letter to yourself and answer it! She gives guidelines. Write in simple language, the way people speak. Use the active voice and make it visual. She looks at Lies. "What about a few illustrations? We really liked last week's drawing for the sugar-and-salt drink."

....

On a Sunday morning Elsie's River is a different place. The streets are quieter. Here and there a family walks to church wearing shiny shoes, suits and ties and hats. Bibles under their arms. It is late winter and a nasty South-Easter blows plastic bags and other rubbish against pavement curbs and wire fences. We drive along Halt Way, past the Day Hospital and the clinic. Posters on lamp posts advertise today's rally: *Join the United Women's Organisation in a celebration of Women's Day at the Municipal Hall.* Lies parks outside the hall. It looks abandoned. Are we even at the right place? A small group of women stand at the door. They look at us suspiciously but confirm that the meeting is happening here; we can go inside to register meanwhile. Inside, in the dim light, we see a giant banner: *The UWO Welcomes you to a Celebration of Women's Day.* Rows of empty seats. A few women wearing headscarves are seated right at the back of the hall. Among them, happily, we recognise Virginia Engel who works for the Food and Canning Workers' Union. She hugs us warmly and we feel better immediately.

An hour and a half later the executive committee of the UWO are seated on the stage. The chairperson welcomes Mama Dora Tamana, who is in a wheelchair, and asks her to open the rally. Everybody rises and we sing *Nkosi Sikelele iAfrika*. I feel the old emotion well up in me as the voices soar and fall. *Morena boleka sechaba sa heso … o se boleku sa heso … sechaba sa Afrika.* The women around us sing with their right fists raised high. I glance at Lies beside me. No, she is also not making the salute. The clenched fist still feels strange to me; extreme and aggressive. I know it is a sign of power and I respect it, but I cannot join in spontaneously.

Now for the speeches. Everything is interpreted into isiXhosa and English, so it takes twice as long. Mama Tamana once again tells the historic tale of the women's march to the Union Buildings. *Strydom you have struck the women. You have struck a rock.* One of the veterans who was there that day, speaks in a creaky voice about how the Boere beat them. She is briefly interrupted by jubilant ululating and cries of "Amandla". The hall is only half full, and young men are in the majority, youth leaders from the townships. Lies and I talk to the small group of people we know from the Observatory branch of the UDF. I remark that very few women from Elsie's River seem to be at the rally. "You are quite right, and that is why we must organise, my sister!" By half past one, huge pots of breyani are carried in and we queue up to eat. The atmosphere brightens and everyone is friendly to us. After lunch people begin heading home. The UWO's first rally is over.

Will I ever forget those rallies of the eighties? After a while I realised I would be at least ninety minutes early if I arrived on time. Is that why people started referring to "African time"?

Among the many small NGO groups that crawled all over the mighty machinery of the state like troublesome ants, was a group of organisations that shared office space in a dilapidated building in Mowbray. In the eighties Mowbray did not have the shine and vibrancy UCT students have given it today. The rundown building was on the corner of Station Road and Main Road, where Grand Bazaars is now. The Health Care Trust was one of the organisations renting an office in it. The HCT had already established a Village Health Worker project in Cala, Transkei, and had appointed me as their full-time field worker in Cape Town. My job was vaguely defined and it was up to me to develop it further. I had to work with trade unions, neighbourhood committees, women's organisations and church groups that needed information and training about health issues. My main task was to "empower" people. Health affects people on an intimate level where we could perhaps make a contribution towards greater awareness of the need for political change. I would report to the HCT trustees, a small group of volunteers; Debbie Budlender and Melanie Alperstein and medical students like Leslie London, Lyn Denny and Nathan.

I will never forget my first day at the office. My first work day ever out of uniform! I wear long pants, a jersey and walking shoes, ready for anything. My stomach churns with nerves. A new challenge. I feel a bit anxious too; what have I let myself in for? Will I fit in? I have already been interviewed by the trustees and they expect a great deal of me, but it is really up to me to define and create my job. I park in a side street and am immediately approached by two homeless people in threadbare clothes who offer to keep an eye on my car. I can't find the entrance in Main Road, but Jeffrey, my car guard, leads me around the corner to a battered trellis gate. Overflowing rubbish bins and broken booze bottles bear witness to wild nights. The building's back door is open and I step inside. The weak neon light reveals a long passage with doors leading off on either side.

It smells of mould and stale cigarette smoke. In a partitioned office a thin man with dreadlocks and an even thinner woman in a shapeless kaftan are sorting through piles of A4 paper and stapling them into folders. I greet them hesitantly, but they barely look up. Luckily, further down the passage I see Neil White, my sole colleague.

"Hi Hester! Welcome to Health Care Trust! Let me show you around." Neil is a young English-speaking doctor I know from Trustee meetings. He works with trade unions on workplace safety issues and does valuable research about conditions in asbestos mines. Neil tells me about his work and explains that he travels a lot and is rarely in the office. "So you will usually have all this space to yourself," he says laughing and points apologetically to the cubby-hole of about three square metres. There is one school desk, one chair and a rusty metal filing cabinet. A few rough planks serving as a bookshelf lean against the wall. "First let me try to find you a chair," Neil says and disappears around the corner. Next we walk to the kitchen area and he switches on the kettle. The sink is filled with dirty coffee mugs, the rubbish bin stinks, and food-encrusted plates cover every surface. All this mess in spite of the threatening message above the sink: "Please wash your own stuff. No one else will!"

Neil rinses two mugs under the tap and we walk back, past the two silent figures I passed earlier. Neil stops and introduces me. "This is Laura and Jamey. They work for the Medical Students Bursary Trust. They send study materials to rural students." The young man smiles broadly. "Welcome to cuckoo land," he says laconically. Laura looks me up and down. She nods … (or did I imagine it?) and returns, expressionless, to her stacking and stapling.

Later Jamey, the dreadlocked Rasta man, gives me a lesson on using the photocopier. After a complicated explanation and a couple of kicks the old beast shudders and spews out a few pages. He smiles: "Best thing is just to call me if you need a copy. The two of us understand one another."

Back at the school desk I open a notebook and begin writing. I make a list of all the organisations and people I have met and then phone them, one by one, asking if they can use my services. Ja, any aspect of health, I explain, although it sounds terribly vague even to me. After a couple of hours I stand up, and this movement sends an enormous rat scurrying across the floor. I shudder and feel homesick for Heideveld where floors were washed every day. Where people knew me and the children in the streets waved at me in a friendly way. It felt like home after five years. Will I ever fit in here?

That Saturday Lies and I arrive at the Mowbray offices at ten o'clock in the morning. The self-appointed caretakers are fast asleep, lost to the world, and do not see us enter the building. We are armed with buckets, brooms, a mop and a bottle of Handy Andy. After I told Lies about the filthy kitchen and office, she offered to help me clean. We tackle the kitchen first. Soaking the food-encrusted plates and cutlery. "It is better to work from the top down," she advises as Trevor walks in. He looks us up and down and bursts out laughing. He works in one of the tiny offices for the Cape Areas Housing Action Committee and we know him from the *Grassroots* Advice Page. "You can laugh all you like," I say sheepishly. "Rather come and help us."

"No, it is just too precious to see the madams washing the floors," he teases. "Heavens, Hester, I am so glad you have arrived. I've been struggling to survive among this group of white lefties. Seems they think the dirtier we are, the more left wing we will appear to the people!"

Today Trevor Manuel is of course an icon. He was part of Mandela's first cabinet and served for a long time as the Minister of Finance. He remains a popular ANC leader. He was on *Pasella* last night. The very model of a well-spoken, successful politician. A man of the world. The interviewer asked him about the old days when he still had to duck and dive from the security police, was detained without trial and had little time to spend with his young family. Those were the days when he handled the housing portfolio for *Grassroots* and was completely comfortable sitting on the carpet with us in our living room in Obs.

In 1982 medical students organised a conference about tuberculosis, ironically called Consumption in the Land of Plenty. I was still working for the HCT but had given notice, having won a bursary to study in England. The trust's offices had moved to a house in Scott Road, Observatory. I was busy handing over my projects to a colleague when Nathan, one of the student trustees, walked in.

Nathan looks terribly serious today. "Come for a quick walk with me," he says. "I'm going to get some lunch at Chippies." I understand immediately that he fears the security police are eavesdropping on our office conversations. We live in a time of oppression. One never knows who else is listening. Nathan says one of his friends was taken in for questioning by the Security Police a few days earlier. Nathan and this friend were both on the committee organising the TB conference. The police had asked Nathan's friend whether he knew Hester van der Walt. "I just wanted to warn you that they are also watching you," Nathan says, concerned.

The moment has come. For a long time now my friends and acquaintances have spent a night or two with us when they need to go into hiding, but now I am also on the list of suspects. A cold shiver runs down my spine. I will be flying to England next week. Or maybe not?

The Diploma in Adult Education at UCT was a great learning curve for me. My dissertation dealt with in-service training and patient education at the Day Hospitals. I was proud of it, but also a little sad that my studies had come to an end.

Clive Millar came to see me afterwards and suggested I consider a master's degree at Manchester University. He reckoned I had a chance of winning a British Council Scholarship. I discussed it with Lies. She was happy for me and encouraged me to apply, but I could see she found the whole idea unrealistic. Shortly after my interview at the British Council offices in the city centre, the dream became a reality. I checked my passport, applied for a visa and began making final plans. This was my chance to become a post-graduate student because Manchester University recognised all my previous nursing diplomas, whereas South African universities required a bachelor's degree.

The idea of a whole year apart from Lies entered the room like a dark elephant standing silently between us. As my date of departure drew closer, Lies grew quieter. She made a blanket coat for me and turned Swazi fabric into a duvet cover for my sleeping bag.

Today, thinking back to that time, I ask her: "How did you really feel about it, Lieske?"

"I remember that just before you left, in the midst of all the commotion, I was lying in the bath one day. And I started to cry, as if for the first time it really hit me that you were leaving and I was staying behind alone."

Last-minute things are packed, goodbyes are said. Nathan has to sit on top of my suitcase to force it shut. We weigh it. Ja, just within the baggage limit. At the airport everything feels surreal. Lies and I said our farewells early this morning and have done our weeping, but my lip trembles again as I walk through customs on my own. Lies and Marian Jacobs stand and wave until I disappear around the corner.

When I started this memoir I made a list of sources I could consult to refresh my memory. The letters Lies and I wrote to each other when I was in England were high on that list. I knew they were somewhere safe with a few of my diaries. I began searching for them yesterday, but they were nowhere to be found. Vanished. Until Lies discovered them on a forgotten shelf beneath my printer. I sit with the faded blue carboard file in front of me. A rectangle of pink paper glued to the flap serves as a label: "Hester's Letters". There is also a small pen-and-ink sketch of me on the flap, and three addresses in Manchester; a record of my search for a suitable place to live in that city.

I open the file. The inside flap is covered with Lies's hand-writing. A detailed record of every letter she received from me, from 15 September 1982 to 15 September 1983. I am deeply moved to see again how she underlined the months, and marked every one that passed, one to twelve, in large letters. There are notes in the margin, about other things that I sent her: *postcard, parcel, cassette tape, tape and soap, card with tea cloths from Holland.* My beloved is any researcher's dream. Data at a glance!

Together we examine the folder, stunned by the number of blue aerograms, the thinnest air letters, each one (an A4 page inside and a third of a page overleaf) crammed with writing about a year in two people's lives. This was years before the existence of e-mails. Lies teases me, as she did then. "Naturally, I wrote more often than you." I have to agree.

Once more I see myself skipping down the wooden stairs in Windsor Road, Manchester, early in the morning after hearing the thud of Bonny's *Guardian* dropping through the slot in the front door. And yes – the post has arrived – two blue letters waiting on the floor! With a singing heart I trot back upstairs to the third floor and my mattress on the floor. I wrap my red and black Swazi duvet around my shoulders and fill my heart with Lieske's news. I am with her, also far from home, somewhere in a little town in the Eastern Cape, struggling to contact village health workers. I reread the letters several times. I look around my strange room. The desk with piles of books and papers. I have been in England for two months and this is my third rented room in an area that reminds me a bit of Observatory. Victorian houses and corner shops. I saw the advertisement for the room on the notice board of Grassroots Bookshop. I telephoned and had to go for an interview. The two women wanted to check what kind of South African I was. I was anxious because I had discovered that the colour of my skin and my accent led to immediate assumptions that I was yet another oppressor. It was to be expected, if you watched the scenes from my country which were broadcast on the TV news night after night.

Another South African was doing the Masters in Adult Education with me, Nomvula, a community worker from Cape Town. We had studied together at UCT for two years and knew each other fairly well. Like me, she had obtained a British Council bursary, and at the airport I helped her redistribute her extra luggage to get it through the boarding gates. On our arrival in Manchester, her attitude towards me changed radically. She looked right through me, as if we had never met before. In a group of less than thirty students this was quite noticeable. More than half of us were foreigners and the university had gone to great lengths to make us feel at home in the city. Nomvula used every opportunity to show how she felt about me, the white Afrikaans oppressor. I endured this pain as a heavy, but unavoidable, burden. When we had to choose areas of specialisation and both chose Community Studies, the atmosphere was so distressing that I changed my selection. It was once again the old dilemma. How can you, as a white South African, escape the collective guilt of your race? For me it has always gone against the grain to use words to explain that I am "different". My difference must be demonstrated through my deeds and attitude. A fellow student from Kenya, Mutua, was a great joy and comfort to me during this time.

He silently observed the situation between Nomvula and me and one day spoke to me about it. After that he went out of his way to include me as "a fellow African".

I pick up the bundle of letters I had written and a small flattened object slips out. A lock of Lies's hair, loosely tied with a white ribbon. These days I am so accustomed to her silver-grey hair, but in 1983 her mane was still light brown, with blonde streaks of sunlight.

> *A lock of hair loosely tied*
> *golden brown and warm against my fingers.*
>
> *Thirty years on it still lives between my fingers.*
>
> *I pick it up from among the blue gossamer letters.*
> *Inhale deeply. It still smells of Lieske.*
>
> *Flowers, warm honey. Honesty.*

I go through the letters chronologically. Like a reel of film that year replays in my mind. Lies completes her studies and goes to work for the Health Care Trust in their East London village health workers project. Endless hardships by train and bus and difficulties with a corrupt project worker. My wanderings in Manchester in search of a place which doesn't feel too alien, where I can spend the year. The longing is tangible in both our letters. Sometimes it is desperate, but mostly there is acceptance that it is just for one year. We console one another and give each other courage. Lies tells me how Lyn came to visit her one afternoon and poured out her heart at the kitchen table. She was in love with a woman and had broken off her engagement to a man. She came to Lies because she intuitively knew she would understand. Lies writes that Lyn is on her way to England and would look me up. I was still sharing a house with a group of young students then, and made up a bed for Lyn on the floor in my room. I was so happy to see her as it was my birthday and the two of us went out for dinner. Afterwards we talked late into the night about acceptance and approval. She introduced me to her favourite poet. A new world opened up before me. It was one of the first really open discussions I had with a third person about my relationship with Lies.

That year in Manchester I became more aware of feminism and began finding my own words for things that had always worried me, like the attitudes and glances of men, and everyday expressions and ideas that stereotyped women. Above all, I found my place in the world as a complete human being, as a woman who is not shy about loving another woman. Even in the struggle, where we always spoke about "standing shoulder to shoulder with men", I was aware that we had not really opened up spaces to be ourselves. It was not by chance that Lyn and I had that conversation in a foreign land.

10

Ithemba

We chose the house at 38 Oxford Street, Observatory, because a sunbeam fell across its wooden floor when we looked through the sash window. I fell instantly in love with the long, narrow house. A passage and one bedroom, then the lounge, then the kitchen and another room and finally a dark little room which led to the bathroom. There was a "patio" outside the kitchen door, a narrow cement strip running alongside the house and bordering the neighbour's six-foot wall. We bought the house for eight thousand rand – a deposit plus monthly payments of eighty rand. Observatory and Salt River became my hunting grounds for secondhand tables and chairs. The front garden measured three by four metres and was covered in long grass. We bought a spade and started clearing it. The little garden underwent a few transformations – a pocket-size lawn, a shrub and a few rose bushes edged with a border of flowers – before we discovered fynbos. We were the youngest homeowners and the first newcomers to the area. Elderly women lived on both sides of us. Then the Parkers. Across the street from us, students rented two houses they called Borborygmi and Flatus; medical students must have lived there at some point. We baptised our home Ithemba which means hope, as in the isiXhosa saying *ithemba alibulali*, "hope does not kill, it brings life". Little did we know that we would live at that address for thirty years.

Mr Stanley Parker tried to take us under his wing immediately. He could barely contain his curiosity. It was just as well that he shared his backyard wall with other neighbours. His wife's elderly mother lived with them. She was an elegant old lady, always dressed in a navy two-piece outfit. Their only pet was a tame hen called Benjy. Mr Parker's greatest pleasure was recounting how he fed his little hen toast and tea at certain times of the day. He kept a vigilant eye on the comings and goings and goings-on at the student houses. "There are boys and girls living there together, you know. I wonder who sleeps with whom. Heh heh …" He was always looking for an excuse to get a closer look. One evening the students arrived home at dusk, amazed to find him crouching in front of their hedge, and staring through the foliage into the window. "What are you looking at, Mr Parker?" He nearly fainted from shock but recovered quickly: "I'm looking for my lost chameleon. I think it might be in your hedge …"

Then there were the Whites, two houses further down the road. Val and John, in their early fifties, and Sharon, their daughter, who at fourteen already knew all about life. Lies started chatting to her and discovered that she liked drawing. Sharon found us interesting because she had never met people like us before. She called us "the intellectuals". She was sceptical about any attempts to reform her. Social workers, whom she'd encountered since she was very young, were her sworn enemies. School was a necessary evil and she could not wait till she was old enough to earn her own money.

At sunset one evening Sharon knocks on our door, she is wearing an anorak and carrying her rucksack. "Just coming to greet yous. I'm on my way to Jo'burg." We coax her inside and can see that she is battling not to cry. Then the story pours out. Her father and mother have been drunk for three days and there is no food in the house. It takes all our powers of persuasion to convince her to spend the night with us. We make up a bed and watch as she hungrily devours a bowl of soup. The next morning she is calmer and decides to stay with us and forget about Johannesburg for now. Sharon gets her Uncle Samie to smuggle her school clothes out of her parents' house on condition that he does not divulge her whereabouts. "I want to give them a real fright this time," she says, determinedly. Lies and I are sick with worry. What if something should happen to her, we would be responsible. She is fifteen and legally still a minor. Are we not obliged to inform the "authorities"? But we have promised Sharon we will tell no one, and she watches us like a hawk. Her trust had been broken so often. She is more streetwise than we are! After a few days her uncle reports that Val and Johnnie have sobered up and are searching everywhere for their daughter. They feel terribly guilty and are beside themselves with worry. Sharon decides to take full advantage of the situation. She might consider returning home, but only until they start drinking again. AA meetings follow and Pa White undergoes a mammoth conversion at the local Methodist Church. Overnight he becomes an elder in the church and an example to all. Ma White plods on, forever the victim with her haggard face and blonde curls.

A few years later, we were fast asleep one night when we were woken by urgent hammering on our door. Val and Samie are on our doorstep, panic-stricken. "Please come immediately Lies, Sharon is in trouble." Lies grabs her shoes and a coat and leaves with them. All the lights are on at the Whites' house; the front door is ajar. Val is crying so hard she cannot speak. Sharon is standing in the cramped little back room, bending over the bed. She is hysterical. On the bed in front of her lies a newborn baby boy. His umbilical cord has been severed and fortunately is not bleeding. The placenta has not been delivered. There is blood everywhere and signs of a wild scuffle. Lies wraps the baby in a towel and helps Sharon to deliver the placenta. Sharon looks confused and terrified. She keeps repeating: "I've done it again, I've done it again." She weeps. Val phones the ambulance. It arrives quickly and takes her to hospital. This was Sharon's second son. The first one was about a year old.

So through love and loss, we became intertwined with that family. Val passed away after a long illness. After a while John left Oxford Street, and Sharon and her children moved to Gauteng. Sometimes, out of the blue, she still phones us.

11

It's better outside

I look in the mirror of yesteryear. The mid-eighties. Just before I turned forty-three. Who was I, then?

Newly home from England. A convert to feminism and inspired by the gospel of community work. I teach adults to read and write. I divide my time between the University of Cape Town and Montagu and Ashton where we do field work, but I am most alive at home in Observatory. I wear loose-fitting clothes, mostly pants and T-shirts. I like to wear blue and ignore the red and brown clothes in my cupboard. I love Lies, the Cederberg and Table Mountain. I hate cigarette smoke. I find family visits difficult. I don't like being reminded about old orthodoxies and do not want to be regarded as an Afrikaner or classified as white. I always have socks and a book at hand and fervently believe true freedom will come one day, but not in my lifetime. On UCT's campus I still feel like an outsider and usually try to provide some balance between my colleague Linda Wedepohl and Rachel Jenkins, our British colleague. Then there is the Montagu community – MAG (meaning power) an acronym for Montagu Ashton Gemeenskapsdienste (or Community Services). I work with Dirk and two radical young project workers who help us to train reading groups on remote farms in the region. I am still involved with *Grassroots* and the Nurses Support Group. Endless meetings. Activists sometimes spend the night because we have a "safe house" in Observatory.

So my life goes on. I long for ordinary everyday humanity, for the day I can rise above the guilt and shame of my heritage. I am so happy to be home with Lies after a long year of separation. I am surrounded by my Obs neighbours, Sharon and the Whites, SPAR and the little pizza place just around the corner.

How big was the cell? There was space for six bunkbeds in two rows of three. A toilet and shower against one wall. Grey blankets. Sheets striped with the words *Department of Correctional Service*. Narrow iron bed. Thin mattress. Small open-shelved bedside cabinet.

After so many years it is still difficult to believe that it happened to me. That there was a knock on our door shortly after five on a clear Cape Town morning in November 1985. That a half-asleep Lies went to open the door. Why Lies? Was I at the other end of the house? That day is a blur in my memory. Perhaps it was shock, or perhaps self-preservation; a way of burying a painful experience. I can still see the fear in Lies's face. "There are two policemen looking for you. I told them you weren't here but they want to search the house." Her helplessness. The terror rising in my breast. And somehow, from some deeper place, the determination to protect her which made me say: "Never mind. I'm coming." I also remember a sense of inviolability. What could they do to me anyway?

The two policemen are already in the sitting room, looking through the telephone numbers in our address book. They speak English badly, with a heavy Afrikaans accent. I reply in Afrikaans. They turn to each other in surprise. The communists even speak Afrikaans now. They search the house systematically. Our bookshelves. My writing table and briefcase. They examine the photographs on the wall and study the faces of our brown and black friends, whispering to each other. The policeman who identified himself as Sergeant Van Zyl shows me his clipboard with a list of names. "Have a look at this list. We are looking for these friends of yours. Where can we find then?" I barely glance at the list and fury wells up in me. Up to now I have controlled my panic by being polite and detached. Correct. "No, Sergeant. I do not know any of them," I say quietly. They grin at each other. I guess they are about my age. Wives and children at home. Van Zyl says I have to go with them. "You can pack a few things; maybe they will keep you overnight." Lies is in tears and I try to comfort her. She wants to know where they are taking me. First to the Mowbray police station and then possibly into detention. I pack a toiletry bag, tracksuit and socks. Outside a strong South-Easter is blowing. An unmarked yellow motorcar is parked across the road. I sit in the passenger seat and Van Zyl gets in the back. Lies stands at the front gate in her dressing gown. I try to reassure her, but barely get the chance to say goodbye.

The Mowbray station is crowded. A cacophony of half-drunk and noisy people. Names are called out. Uniforms. I'm already invisible. Just one more suspect. Van Zyl takes me to a small office and orders the constable to take my fingerprints and photograph me; this is apparently a formality before he takes me to be detained at Pollsmoor. This cannot be true. I make an effort to speak to them rationally. Why? What is the charge against me? No, they do not need a charge-sheet. I am being detained in terms of the State of Emergency because I pose a threat to the security of the state. Provisionally for two weeks, and thereafter it will be reviewed every two weeks.

Pollsmoor Prison lies in a beautiful valley between green mountains on the road to Muizenberg. In an ordinary suburb with family homes and crescent streets. A jail. A prison. A world apart. There is a separate prison for white prisoners. The security police take me to the section for white women, where female warders in brown uniforms await me. One searches my overnight bag. She examines every item and lists it on a form. She counts the money in my purse and records the total. We speak Afrikaans. Only the necessary words. She does not look me in the eye, as if we are both shy, ashamed to be part of this probing ritual. Or is it just my imagination? It's just part of her daily job. To lock up terrorists and keep society safe.

I am locked up in a communal cell with five other women, also so-called political prisoners. I have met Yvonne Shapiro before. Her family is famous in leftist circles, particularly her mother. She embraces me and introduces me to the others who give me a friendly "welcome". The conversation goes in circles: what do they want from us, what is happening in the news, what is happening outside? Lyn Garwen is a teacher at a school in the townships. Virginia Zweigental is a medical student. She and Josette Cole are involved in church-related community work. And Debora Patta, the beautiful Debs? Probably a journalist. I am the oldest. The only Afrikaans speaker. We are all a bit confused. In limbo. Glad we have each other for support, a small circle of solidarity in a hostile environment. At four-thirty in the afternoon the cell is unlocked and we are taken to a small dining room next to the cell. Sliced bread. Margarine. Peanut butter. Apricot jam. Tea. Afterwards we are locked up again for the night.

I sit on my bed. Watch how each displaced person falls silent. Some keep busy. Josette and Virginia play a word game. Lyn reads. There are a few books in the cell, but for the first time in my life I get no pleasure from reading. Thoughts race through my head. What will Lies do now? I know she is thinking about me and she must be worried sick. Breathe. Stay calm. The cell grows quiet. Far away a dove coos. Then harsh voices scream at one another further down the corridor. Is somebody being tortured? There are rumours that thousands of people across the country are already in detention, and more are being detained. Yvonne received a message that all detainees would embark on a hunger strike soon, in protest.

And yet, the days pass. After a while a deadly dull routine develops. When the warder unlocks the door for breakfast at six-thirty, the cell must be neat and tidy. Beds made. I notice how small acts of resistance help us express our powerlessness and rage. Like refusing to get out of bed, or stand up, when the warders enter the cell. The warders are awkward and don't know how to deal with this bunch of English women. The young warder calls her senior, who speaks to me in Afrikaans. I shudder and feel contaminated. I can see she wants to use me as her interpreter and intermediary. My way of resisting is to insist on normality, because I am just an ordinary person who simply does not belong here. I ask for my knitting. They will find out if it is permitted. The warder returns in half an hour. My cell mates are intrigued by this interaction. No, knitting is definitely against the rules. No sharp objects are allowed!

Breakfast is mieliepap. I am the only one that grew up with it. It's part of my culture and I remember how Ma made it. Sometimes, in the backyard, I begged Anna for some of her suurpap.

One by one we are summoned for interrogation. There are two men from the security police. Dressed in civvies. A stack of files is piled on the desk in front of them. A woman warder is seated at the back of the room. My heart pounds in my throat and I feel slightly dizzy. The start of a migraine. Then instinct kicks in. A calm comes over me and I decide to jump in first. "I hope that today you will tell me why I am being held here, because I have absolutely no idea and it is a waste of everyone's time." They look at each other and smile, slightly sheepishly. Slightly uncertain? "No Miss. It does not work like that. We want to know everything about you." I suspect they themselves have no idea why I am here. They are just fishing. Poor devils. Just small cogs in the great security machine.

The hunger strike starts today. All meals are returned untouched. We feel part of the countrywide protest. The nurse, wearing a prison services uniform with epaulettes, comes to address us. She refuses to give one of my fellow detainees her anti-depressant medication. The rule is simple: if you don't eat, you can't have your medicine. This gives me a fright. It could have serious consequences. We are all upset. We force ourselves to drink water.

The next day is my birthday, 12 November. I am tearful from early morning. The warder brings me the clothes Lies sent from home. Everything is brand new, packed in a pretty new basket. I realise it is her way of giving me presents. Colourful tops and undies. Later that day we are taken to the visiting area for visiting hour. The vast space is divided into narrow cubicles with glass windows through which you and your visitor may talk.

Lies smiles bravely, but I cry so hard I can't speak. In between sobs I try to reassure her. I am okay. Really. She says Sharon sends birthday greetings. Everyone does. She talks about the latest antics of Stoffel Prinsloo, our cat. She shows me birthday cards friends sent with her, but the warder stops her. No messages from outside. And in any case, visiting time is over. We press our palms together on either side of the glass partition, and I convince myself some warmth reaches me.

On the third day of the hunger strike I realise things are going dangerously awry. I am the oldest in our cell and, what is more, a nurse. Emotions are running high. Why would we want to put our health at risk and punish ourselves even more than they are already doing? I talk to Lyn. She agrees and we convince Yvonne, Josette and Ginny to start eating something. We have to build up our strength and ensure that our cell mate gets her medication again.

The days drag by. After a fortnight detention can be extended for another two weeks. This is what happened to Lyn. Every day we have two exercise periods when we can walk on the tarred surface of the outside courtyard. No plants or soil, but I can see the sky and watch the clouds go by and feel the wind on my cheeks. Two rock pigeons are building a nest in the gutter way up high on the wall. Our little group of "inmates" gets to know each other well. Everyone's sorrows and doubts and everyone's unique talents, such as storytelling. Virginia's study material is another source of inspiration. Each one of us wants to be strong for the others. One day, while we are walking in the courtyard, our cell is searched. Debora's diary is seized and she has to sign a confiscation form. Right away I tear up everything I have written and think back to how Van Zyl paged through my address book on the morning of my detention.

On my fourteenth day in detention I wake up crying. Too scared to hope, but hopeful nonetheless. And, yes, a message arrives instructing me to collect my belongings as I am being discharged. My five cell mates hug me tightly, and we weep together. They are happy for me, but sad to be left behind. As I walk down the passage they sing *Malibongwe* for me, the old praise song for courageous women. At the end of the passage I catch a glimpse of Lies. We wave hysterically, but my official discharge must be completed first. The filling of forms. The return of all my possessions and signatures to acknowledge receipt. And, no, I may not join my friends yet, I will be discharged from the Wynberg Police Station. I am transported to Wynberg in the back of a police van with four young girls from Grassy Park. We are total strangers, but embrace each other as comrades. Lies follows right behind the van with Naeema and Melanie. They are holding huge bunches of flowers and just before we were locked into the van, they threw each of us a flower. The constables in charge did not know where to look. The world outside is glorious. The mountain has never looked so beautiful. So many voices. So many people. Bewilderment. Anxiety. Who is watching us? How safe am I in my own home? The following weeks are a time of confusion and looking-over-my-shoulder anxiousness.

Pollsmoor. Was it a turning point in my life, and if so, in what way? Before my detention I saw my role in the struggle as being one of support only, and thus very limited. I was definitely not in the league of the so-called senior activists who attended up to three meetings a night and made public appearances. Now I had suddenly become a sort of struggle celebrity. Unwillingly. Convinced that I hadn't really done anything much and did not deserve the honour. Forever guilty? All the same, my whole world was turned upside down for several months. My doctor even wanted to admit me to a psychiatric clinic, but Lies and I decided to go away for a while instead. Our beloved Obs home had been invaded and pawed and defiled, and in all likelihood bugged, by enemy forces. We spent a few days in Kleinmond, at a friend's holiday house. But the contamination came with us. I slept badly and felt jumpy all the time. My thoughts kept returning to the two women still incarcerated in our cell. One of them, I suspected, battled with anorexia. I still did not feel free. One day, in Athlone, my car wouldn't start. My first thought was that someone had tampered with it while installing some listening device.

Lies was suffering as much as me. Her pain was worse, because she had opened the door to the police. "In Holland during the Second World War my father hid in the cellar every time we heard the sound of the German soldiers' heavy boots. They took all Dutch men away to compulsory labour camps. One day they hammered on our door incessantly. Eventually my pa said to my ma: 'Oh just go and open it.' But she didn't. She waited and after a while they went away. But I opened the door." On the morning of my arrest, as soon as I was taken away, she crossed the road to our neighbour Willie Hofmeyr to tell him what had happened. His advice was to tell as many people as she could. Especially people in the Netherlands and England.

The Detainees' Parents Support Committee helped her. Like someone who has lost a loved one, she told the story over and over to anyone willing to listen. During that period thousands of people were detained without trial all over the country. The headline of a report in the *Cape Times* of 9 November 1985 read: *87 held, 15 released.*

Lies came to Pollsmoor every day, supposedly to bring me clean clothes. I think it helped her feel closer to me. I can just imagine how she disarmed the reception staff with her characteristic charm, which does not let up until you give her your full attention. In the cell everyone teasingly called me "the best dressed detainee in the Western Cape". Together we examined every seam and hem for hidden messages. One day we were allowed to receive a small carton of Bulgarian yoghurt from Lies. Adding a teaspoon to milk, I began making our own yoghurt. The human spirit always finds a way to beat the system.

The worst thing about this time was not being able to write anything down. I couldn't keep a journal, in case it fell into the wrong hands. Going through my old diaries the other day, I came across a folded plastic bag. A few notes and handmade birthday cards. Newspaper cuttings. Letters of support and love. An envelope with a few photographs from my colleague Linda Wedepohl, inside a UCT envelope. A handwritten warning on the back read: "They may have dropped a bug in your house." The bag also contains a number of yellowing pages torn from a small notebook. A couple of clumsy attempts at ballpoint line drawings. I recognise my style. A few words in pencil: "It's better outside. Second Wednesday." The next page contains an attempt at a self-portrait, with a caption by Lies: "Threats from left and right. Note the shoulders." The shoulders are hunched up high and disproportionately large. There is a quotation from Breytenbach: "Do yourself a selfish favour; if you want to remain whole, recognise the humanity of your enemy." Sunday, 1 December. Kirstenbosch. A few line drawings which attempt to capture the shape of plants and a note at the bottom: "Here it is easy to imagine that all life is one."

The packet with newspaper cuttings has been sealed for twenty-seven years. Every time we moved or tidied up, it was kept with the books. Unopened. Safe. Like Pandora's box. But now the memories have escaped and old feelings return. And yet the feelings are more muted, like the memory of pain. Dull, without a sting. For a long time I would not allow myself to write about those times. Anxious that "they" would read my words and perhaps find some reason to punish me and others. Self-censorship. They succeeded in that. That is why I am writing about it now, so that everybody who wants to know will know, today and in the future, how ridiculous and petty oppression is, how many layers of oppression there were, and how even the tiniest little cog like me experienced it.

12

From Cape Town to McGregor

Freedom did arrive. Sooner than I dared imagined. Yes, in my lifetime!

On the parade among thousands of people, I stood and waited for Madiba. When he finally appeared I could hardly see him through my tears, I could barely hear him, because of the wild rejoicing around me. Then the first democratic elections. A voting queue at Mowbray's town hall that wound around the entire block. The people, total strangers, sharing umbrellas in the drizzle. United in euphoria. We had made history. Finally our votes counted. Shortly afterwards, disillusionment set in. There had always been political power struggles between the comrades, the battle for seniority, the self-promotion, the competition to be included in lists. I chose not to see it because my heart was loyal, until the day my body fled without my head playing any part in the decision.

Leaving Pick n Pay in Rondebosch that day, I walk slap-bang into a group of people gathered around a table. Behind the table I recognise a few comrades, people I know from the UDF days, now wearing new ANC T-shirts. A large ANC flag covers the table. This is where you can sign up for party membership. When I came to, I was two blocks away outside the book shop. Still carrying my heavy shopping bags; out of breath. My body had fled instinctively.

I try to make sense of my previous life. Of my political

evolution; from a highly involved, guilt-ridden, duty-bound, fix-the-world city dweller to an awareness that that kind of activism of the development set, that time of my life, has come to an end. That my role is more modest, that my waning strength can be used differently now. That upliftment – I always loathed that word – is unnecessary, and patronising to boot.

Round about the same time I became aware of my spiritual needs again. One Sunday during a midday nap, half asleep, I hear a man's voice on the radio. The presenter asks the man about his work and he speaks about Temenos, a retreat centre in McGregor. "But how do you see your role," the interviewer asks. The man laughs shyly: "I see myself as a spiritual midwife." So we find ourselves in Temenos for a weekend away and meet Billy Kennedy, the charming midwife who introduces us to the techniques of meditation. Meditation, where I search for my energy again in the spiritual, the invisible. I read Jack Korndorf. We meet Johann Verster, a friend of Billy's.

It is also a time of returning to the things of the body, of the earth. I start baking bread. Create handicrafts. Fall in love all over again with the simplicity and purity of the platteland. We spend more time in Temenos.

This new phase started almost spontaneously. With a turning away from the ANC and activism, and a questioning, a sort of gut feeling. At the time I was working for the Medical Research Council. There too I was aware of a power struggle to control the parastatal organisation. There was a constant scrabbling for status, for research grants and ongoing attempts at "restructuring" to get the right people into key positions. I grew tired, sick and tired, of making endless applications for funds to do work that would support nurses. Tired and sad and ill. Burnt out.

In addition, Lies was anxious about the studio she was building in our loft. A builder we once trusted kept putting our project on hold and produced inferior work. She worried about damp, it was the start of the rainy season and the mould blooms on the walls of my room were multiplying.

I remember my own growing despair closing in like the walls of a tunnel. My initial excitement about a project that would support nurses, so they in turn could improve patient care, was systematically eroded by a dark feeling of powerlessness. Daily the office walls at the Medical Research Council closed in on me more tightly. My colleagues were all busy with never-ending re-structuring processes. Gossipy whispers covered the walls like the mould in my home. Piles of guidelines for new projects and requests for articles to be published in the "right" international journals covered my desk like noxious weeds. Eventually I sat as close to the window as I could, where I could at least see the blue sky and clouds. As far away as possible from the rest of the building with its files filled with all my failed attempts at collecting funding for my research. I began fleeing the building to work in the closest coffee shop in Tygerberg. In a shopping centre that had long lost its glamour for me, I sat reading and writing, trying to make sense of the darkness within and around me, and my inability to find the light, to try to build up some enthusiasm for something again. My fire and my light were extinguished. I remember it felt as if I had to drag myself through deep sand, from one meeting to the next. My young student intern looked at me reproachfully, as if his only chance for a doctorate depended on me. The person I reported to had also begun to lose hope. He just wanted to move to Canada or somewhere in Scandinavia, as he had his own problems with head office. His work was questioned too, and considered not politically correct, but at least he had his respected statistical prowess to fall back on. All I had was the soft science of feelings that ultimately influence behaviour. But how do you measure that? And how do you record it in statistically provable columns and charts? I still preferred doing qualitative analyses by hand and was hesitant about entrusting all my data to computers.

I remember the isolation of that time. My university colleagues were sympathetic and wanted to help, but in the end I had to admit to myself that I was tired of fighting, and tired of begging for money to turn my dream job into reality. At work everyone was too busy defending their own corners, even those who believed in me. What saved me during that time was the simple pleasure of making bread. Flour, water, salt and yeast which I kneaded into dough and baked into chewy honest loaves. Something I could swallow, digest and eliminate. With funding proposals I was totally powerless.

My friends suggested that I attend a retreat. For the first time in my life I was officially running away, fleeing the narrow tunnel my working life had become.

I book in at Temenos for two weeks. It is early winter, but McGregor is far colder than Cape Town. Mornings are icy and temperatures drop to freezing right after dusk. I left home in a hurry and did not bring enough warm clothes. I smell of smoke and wood fires. Fortunately I manage to get the fire going in the hearth, at the expense of much smoke and many blocks of Blitz. I sit on the floor in front of the fire. My nose and eyes burn from the smoke, but rather that than the tears I've shed lately. It is strange to be here by myself, alone in Carmel cottage. Last time I was here with Lies and we fell in love with it. It is a sanctuary for city dwellers. A safe haven carefully created by Billy, a lover of beauty. He calls his garden "the garden of the beloved". I smell wet soil, a lavender bush outside the door and the last roses of autumn that someone placed on my table. I wrap Billy's rust-coloured blanket around my shoulders. It is a little scratchy but still comforting. Suddenly I feel like a buffalo. Earlier today I drew the buffalo card from the Native American Medicine Cards. Whenever I am seized by panic about the future, I force my thoughts to return to the here and now. The smell of the fire. The warmth on my left shoulder and leg. My warm cheek. The brown pelt around my shoulders. The roses' sweet scent.

The smell of the roofbeams and thatch in this friendly hut. For a few moments I grow calm. The church bells chime six o'clock and it is time for meditation in The Well. Wrapped in the blanket, I enter the womb-like space. Dark red walls and floor. Candles in earthenware pots surrounding a central pool of water which bubbles softly. The scent of frankincense and myrrh. A large fire burning in the fireplace against the furthest wall. Cushions and rugs to sit or kneel on. I sit close to the water, overwhelmed by so much protection. As my eyes adjust to the dim light, I notice an image on the floor tile in front of me: A hide and two eyes. The head of a buffalo. I remember what I read on the card earlier:

> *If you have drawn the Buffalo card you may be asked to honour the sacredness of your pathway even if it brings you sadness. This time will bring serenity amidst chaos if you pray for calmness and give praise for the gifts you already have.*

I remember that experience with gratitude. After the first week I had gained some perspective, but it took another week of conversations and self-examination before I came to a decision; even though I was only 57 and would receive a tiny pension, I was going to resign from my job. In the end my happiness and health was worth more than money, status or ego. What is more, I did not have to single-handedly save the country's health care services!

It was a time of big decisions; within months, I had resigned from my job, we had sold our house and signed a lease in McGregor. Suddenly life was new. A house to rent, a café to manage, spinach to pick – speckled with almond blossoms. It was as if I sat under a pear tree and the ripe fruit fell into my lap. No salary, but abundance everywhere.

Thinking back to that time, eleven years ago, I am surprised that it seems so distant. Has the texture of imprisonment, a darkening tunnel, an inability to move, left me completely? Thank God, yes! I realise now that I was depressed; that I was sick and tired of five years in an industry where I had to fight for my space inch by inch. Where, from the start, I was the strange fish in the pond. Of course, there was also the excitement of doing my own research, and the opportunity to achieve my doctorate as part of my job and the satisfaction and insights that came with that. Yet even this was only possible with the help of academics outside the structures of the Medical Research Council.

Something inside of me has also shifted. During this decade in McGregor I let go of some of my innate striving to identify and open up spaces for other people. I believe it is a kind of illness, one with a characteristically sticky texture; my fix-the-world sickness and my atonement sickness. I have left that behind. Careful, my inner voice warns, it can return at any time. Yet from where I am now, here in this clearing, the space is astonishingly vast. I still create cosy corners to retreat into, where it's warm and safe. But these are friendly shelters. My little red room, two metres by two metres, with its narrow bed, handmade bedside cabinet and desk and bookshelves. A Persian carpet beneath my feet. A wall niche with a radio and Vicks. Two windows with blue frames from Oudtshoorn that look out at the Sonderend Mountains and my old musk rose bush on her trellis in a bed filled with blue sage. Vusi the ginger cat and Pixel the dog, with her skittish limbs, snuffly nose and velvety eyes, pop in every now and then to check I am still around. The textures of the past, the dark anxiety and oppression, were the antitheses of all this light. Was the light possible without the darkness? Did the dark force me to move, to throw caution to the wind? I think so.

....

These days I feel grounded and my feet are firmly planted on the earth. At the same time there is a new lightness in my step, as if an old burden has fallen from my shoulders. I wear handmade clothes, a jersey I knitted myself and a short skirt Lies made for me on her sewing machine. All my clothes are made from natural fabrics; wool, cotton or silk. Our home was hand built according to our design and taste. It grew organically from the land – on a patch of earth that initially felt far too large to cultivate ourselves. Now it still feels spacious but is filled with bounty. Nature is all around me. A paperbark acacia has finally, after twelve years, broken through the shale rock and sent its roots into the clay soil. Sun and shadow. Seasons. The full moon shining through the window on my face. Flames in the fireplace and in the woodfired oven. Lies is the stoker and I the baker and together we make perfect handcrafted bread. The textures of my body change every day. Contours relax and soften. My skin feels more and more like old soft clothes that fit comfortably, although my muscles and joints protest if I move too fast for my current flexibility and heart's capacity. And these days my head says: "Slow down, you are in too much of a hurry for me."

13

The Kimberley wedding

They said he wasn't marriage material, but here he is in front of the altar, a flower on his lapel, the flushed-with-pride groom, father of the moon-faced one-year-old on his arm. Father and son, the priest and the rest of us are waiting for the bride. The organist warbles out *Ave Maria*, giving it an unusual rhythm. A murmur ripples through the seated guests. She's here! The organist quickly switches to the first chords of the wedding march. Two angelic children enter first, each armed with a basket of rose petals that come all the way from our friend Poena's garden. They sprinkle a carpet of petals for the bride's feet. And here she is finally, on the arm of her proud Pa, in his finest dark church suit. She is radiant. Alta, child of my oldest brother, Roussouw. A mature bride of almost forty. The congregation stands and cranes for that first glimpse of the long cream bridal gown, handsewn by her aunts and mother-in-law.

In my mind's eye I can still see Alta as a teenager. Sturdily built and slightly awkward. Her mother's clever, responsible, oldest child. Her younger brother was the carefree blond prince with his father's large blue eyes and Cupid's bow mouth. Alta inherited her mother Dina's full figure as well as her profession as a mathematics teacher. A rare species, still hard to find on the platteland. I last saw Alta a decade ago, when she was nearly thirty; even that was a dangerous age for an Afrikaans girl, because everyone wanted to know when she would marry. Alta was a schoolteacher in a small Karoo town then. Involved with the church's youth work. Sweet natured and still slightly shy.

Then, out of the blue, almost two years ago my sister Anetha told me Alta was pregnant. And what is more, the man was presumably not marriage material. He was Alta's colleague, also a teacher, and they both lived at the school hostel. I thought it was wonderful news, but it was a great shock for Alta's mother. I gave Dina some time to process her daughter's news and phoned her a few weeks later. We chatted about the weather and everyone's health before I asked her whether it was true that another grandchild was on the way.

"Ja, it is true and I am still shocked! If she was twenty I could understand it, but at her age she should know better." Yes, Dina said, she had met "the male" and was not impressed at all. "To make matters even worse he is English, and you know I can't speak English at all." I tried to reassure Dina. "You will just have to accept it. Alta is an adult and she will know what to do. Alles sal regkom!" Lies and I started knitting for the baby right away. A beautiful little multi-coloured coat and a blanket from Elizabeth Zimmerman's book. It was almost as if we wanted to make the child and his parents feel extra welcome in the family. Little Ernie was born in October and my brother said the headmaster had fortunately given permission for the three to continue living at the school. "In separate sections of the hostel of course, but Alta and the baby have been given an extra room. It's a relief, as there had been talk of suspension." Good heavens, I wondered, were we still living in Victorian times?

The long trip from McGregor to Kimberley started the night before the wedding. We asked our friend Arjan to give us a lift to Worcester. He arrives at Poena's door at six o'clock in the evening. We drive through the green vineyards of our valley with the rain falling heavily during an unusually wet winter. Through Robertson. Past mountain ranges and rocky ridges, the last bright pink vygies and the spears of aloes to the N1 petrol station outside Worcester where all the busses stop. Another hour to wait, and hardly anywhere to sit. This is how most South Africans travel. Bus trips have a distinctive culture and present a true picture of our rainbow nation. White faces are rare. Just us, the oldest, and a few young people in jeans and hoodies, carrying backpacks. A group of Nigerians or Ethiopians are travelling with enormous striped bags. One or two slim men with exquisitely chiselled profiles guard the bags while the others go in search of snacks and cigarettes. Traders? In what? Perhaps contraband, my story-brain says. Our nation is on the move. Busses to the Eastern Cape to Durban and to George. It is already very dark. Lies, as usual, has started chatting to a few fellow travellers. The men assure us: "No Ma, he is on his way. This bus is always on time." Finally we take our seats on the bus, snugly side by side, me with my pillow and blanket. Our rucksack contains two delicious sandwiches and a mysterious jam jar half-filled with straw-coloured liquid. Our friend Annie said no one should attempt a long distance bus trip without a nightcap. "Just take a little whisky in a hipflask, my dear!" We have no hipflask, hence the jam jar. Like naughty children we sip the hard tack. Quite strong neat! A bit of bottled water to dilute it and we each take two big mouthfuls, surreptitiously, because booze is not permitted on the bus. As if anyone is going to check up on two oumas.

And now here we are in the old Methodist Church in Kimberley for the wedding of Alta and Ernie, "the male". In spite of all her reservations, Dina has made all the arrangements herself; from designing the invitations to arranging the corsages and buttonholes. For me it is also a kind of family reunion, because we seldom get together. We have come from all across the country: Witbank, Secunda, Welkom and Mossel Bay. Dina had booked us all into the Horse Shoe Inn, a motel in Kimberley. After all the congratulations outside the church we go back to the motel's entertainment area, the Pool Room. Dina has planned the table seating carefully. In-laws on one side. Unmarried young cousins and their partners on one side. Luckily Lies and I are included with the Van der Walt sisters and their spouses. Children race around between the tables gleefully. Outside thunder claps and hail pelts down. Sherry at the door, juice on the tables, champagne for the toasts and a cash bar for everything else. A buffet dinner with tables groaning with meat dishes. Boere Baroque at its best, punctuated by the inevitable sexist jokes delivered by the master of ceremonies, the bride's uncle.

This is the first of a number of weddings of my nephews and nieces, and the only one I don't attend alone. Lies and I are here together because Alta's marriage is unusual. Even so, the traditions around weddings remain strange to me. Lies and I exchange glances every now and then during the festivities. A still point. I know that later when we are alone there will be much to talk about and I am grateful all over again that we chose each other fifty years ago and still make the same choice every day.

14

Being together, being ill

We've walked the road so long my lamb
step by step and hand in hand
so free-and-easy and so full of joy
a hester and a lies

we walk the same road my lamb
but sometimes just sometimes my lamb
my pathway takes a turn
where follow me you can't

I walk the illness path my lamb
gasping for air alone
it gets dark and constricted my lamb
every footstep an effort of will

that is when I am afraid my lamb
for myself but also for you
that is when you are afraid too my lamb
for yourself but also for me

we've walked the road so long my lamb
open eyed for thorns along the way
and still we learn to trust each other even more my lamb
with one another's pain

[with thanks to Amanda Strydom]

In the lamplight, the small room looks like a
Rembrandt painting. The only beam of light falls on
the thin figure in bed, propped up against a mountain
of pillows. Her nostrils are flaring in a bid to take
in more air. The whistle of her tight chest is clearly
audible above the soft hissing of gas lamps and the
tropical night sounds of frogs and crickets in the
garden outside the nurses' house. Lies sits beside the
bed and tries to cool the patient's feverish face with
a wet cloth. She is worried and feels powerless. Two
missionary doctors, Piet and Evert, and a nurse,
Dith, deliberate in muted tones in the next room. The
standard treatment for asthma has provided little relief
for their colleague Hester's bronchial spasm. They talk
about "status asthmaticus". It seems the adrenaline and
theophylline injections have only increased her heart
rate.

It is the late nineteen-sixties, in a remote mission hospital in what was then called Venda, now an area in Limpopo province. The nearest large hospitals are in Pretoria and Johannesburg.

Piet phones a colleague in Pretoria, a Dutch lung specialist, for advice. Dith returns to the sickroom and speaks quietly to Lies: "What do you think, shouldn't we try to contact Hester's parents?"

I can still hear the way Dith pronounced my name and for a minute I am back in that room and watching the scene unfold as if from a great distance. I see how shocked Lies looks. Tears roll down her cheeks. She holds me in her arms to try to keep me sitting as upright as possible. I stretch out my hand to Dith and she comes closer. I try my best to speak to her in between frantic gasps for air but barely manage to get the words out: "Dith … you know, don't you … about Lies and me …?" Dith, who is also sad, nods understandingly: "Don't worry girl, just relax."

I often wonder about that moment. Was it a kind of confession? Like the people around me that distressing night, I too felt that my final hours had come. My relationship with Lies was still, at that time, a deep secret which only we knew about. I think my attempt to tell Dith about us was a way of involving her. Of saying to her: "Comfort Lies if I am not around anymore. Take care of her, she is precious and vulnerable."

In the weeks that followed I slowly recovered until I was strong enough to travel. Lies took me to Bloemfontein where I was treated by the lung specialist who had cared for me during my student days.

Since then, to a great extent, I have outgrown my asthma. Thanks to modern preventative medicine, I seldom have an "attack". There are however certain triggers, such as the common cold or flu which I have to treat carefully so they don't get out of hand. Recently I had two summer colds close together that resulted in prolonged constriction and fatigue. And so Lies took me to see the new doctor in our town.

We sit on the bench outside her consulting rooms. "Come in," the doctor calls. Her brown eyes smile. I rise and Lies asks hesitantly: "Do you mind …?" "Of course not. You are the significant other and you have every right to be here."

The doctor listens to me and examines me with the familiar, gentle but down-to-earth frankness of a true healer. She allays our worst fears, explaining that heart attacks present differently in men and women. "I want to find out what this tiredness means so I am going to send you to a specialist for tests. And these moles; they will require a biopsy." She answers our questions with authority, thoroughness and sensitivity. And as usual, gratitude for this much kindness reflects on my trembling lower lip.

She looks at me. "Are you scared?" She puts a reassuring arm around me. I shake my head and confess that I come from a family that cries easily. "Don't worry," she says. "I am the same, my husband always says I cry for no reason during movies."

Then I suddenly remember the stories doing the rounds in town that the new doctor herself had suffered a heart attack. "Yes," she admits and shows us the scars of the operation underneath her summer top. "A triple bypass, almost five months ago." This draws us even closer together, this radiant young woman of barely forty and I. Another wounded healer.

And Lies's illnesses?

"Ag no!" Lies cries. I look up from where I am mixing bread dough and see her stagger to the closest chair and collapse into it. "What's wrong?" I ask. She sits bent over, peering with concern at her left foot and the big toenail she recently treated for a fungal infection. When I come closer I see the same toenail sticking up at an unnatural angle. She caught it on something and now it has come loose, uncovering the new nail growing underneath.

Lies is pale. "Wait here," I say, "I'll get a plaster." When I return with plasters and bandages, she is tugging at the old nail. Gruesome. She insists on bandaging the toe herself, perhaps afraid that I might pull it too tight. I pass her the roll of plasters and go to fetch the scissors. When I get back she is lying back in the chair, completely limp. Unconscious! I call her name but get no response. Is she breathing? I loosen her clothes and take her pulse, it is beating slowly. Am I imagining it or is she turning blue? Panic seizes me. A million questions fly through my head. What if she should die? Who can I call? Our neighbours might not even be home. I call her name and slap her cheeks and suddenly she opens her eyes.

She looks around in a daze. "Why are you hitting me?" she asks, upset. I weep with relief. "I was completely gone. I suppose I fainted," she says surprised and suddenly remembers her toenail.

That is Lies. Because she is so tall, and such a feet-on-the-ground pragmatist, her sensitivity always comes as a surprise. I remember her story about her first day as a student nurse in the Bloemfontein National Hospital. She reported for duty in her brand-new, crisp-white uniform at a quarter to seven. In the sister's office, the night shift staff were briefing the day shift.

"The nurse was deathly pale and looked so tired after her twelve hour shift. She spoke about drips infusing into tissues. One of the patients had been very restless and had fallen out of bed, so she had to call the doctor. Everything looked so bad. Suddenly I began feeling light-headed. I left the room and went to stand in the passage. Fortunately there was a long bench and I sat down with my head between my knees. I was so ashamed when the nurses walked out of the office and saw me sitting there. One brought me a medicine glass of sal volatile smelling salts. The sister just smiled and said I should go to the kitchen to help with the patients' breakfasts. To think I fainted before I had even seen my first patient!"

And yet this same woman became a professional nurse in the operating theatre of the Red Cross Children's Hospital. Working with the famous Barnard brothers' heart team, no less. Ja, Lies is both sensitive and strong. Our sicknesses and ailments are very different. I am prone to chest troubles and have been ill more often. But in her younger years Lies suffered from dark moods that at first left me utterly helpless. In retrospect, it was a form of depression which we had no words for then. And also no treatment. The moods arrived, lasted a few days, and left again of their own accord. Eventually I realised I could not do much to help her. I could only be there and afterwards, when she felt better, she sometimes told me what had caused her such anguish.

It was only much later, when we were middle-aged, that we separately, each in our own time, met therapeutic psychologists who helped us grow in self-understanding. Lies was way ahead of me and I could see how much she benefited from the lengthy and to me slightly mysterious process of intimate talking-and-listening with a stranger. Later, during a crisis which left me wondering what life was really all about, I had to overcome my fear that therapy would change me so drastically that it would drive Lies and I apart and make us strangers to one another. How deeply the fear of change is embedded in our psyche! The desire to cling to old patterns at all costs, as if change is not a natural part of life. In the end we both found that our experience of therapy brought us closer to each other. We learnt to understand our old wounds – those places which will always remain vulnerable – and now we can even tease each other and laugh together if one of us sees the other's "soft spot" approaching from far away.

Recently my latest bout of flu, which resulted in a closed chest, coincided with the sudden decline of our elderly ginger cat Vusi. I was so ill I was barely aware of Vusi until all at once I noticed that he, like me, was struggling to breathe. I helped Lies to place him on a soft blanket in his cat basket. I watched her drive off alone to the nearest vet in our neighbouring town. Hours later she returned with the news that Vusi had cancer and was unlikely to survive the treatment.

We mourned together. Lies was inconsolable. "This is too much. You and Vusi. If I have to remain behind alone one day … I can't even think about it." I saw her fear and wanted to take it away. I heard myself say: "Ag never mind, I promise you I won't go first, no matter what!" She smiled through her tears. "You better not, because believe me, I will cause havoc on my own!"

Fortunately growing old is a chronic condition that happens so gradually you get used to it by degrees. Until one day you look into a strange mirror by accident and see your ma. These days I often see my father's hands fumble, for no good reason, as they reach for something. Or I catch myself sitting on the edge of the bed to dry my feet, just like Ma used to do. Normally I am hardly aware of the fact that Lies is older than me, because she is young in spirit and body. No one ever believes her true age. Both her parents had rheumatism and she is also prone to stiff joints and muscles. Like most nurses, Lies is sceptical about medical treatment when it comes to herself. She would far rather try alternative or so-called complementary remedies, and there are many to choose from in our town, which is known as a "free-range old age home". There is literally a cure for every ailment on your nearest street corner. Although well-intentioned, it can irritate me. One is almost afraid to admit that you have been to see a doctor or are taking antibiotics. There's a good chance that a neighbour will tilt her head and ask: "And you're OK with that?"

What will the end be like and how will the one left behind survive? We sometimes think about the last stanzas of *Later*, a poem by Simon Carmiggelt, which Herman van Veen sings so beautifully, and know that even death is part of life.

I promise you, that I will
learn to be attentive
and that I will try often
to make you laugh

laugh like an old lady
who has had her say
and while she is laid out
has no cause to feel ashamed

well, well, well that's how it will be
and then we'll both die quietly
on a Thursday in March
together – that's what I believe

and when our earthly remains
become one with the soil
from you a flower will bloom
the face of a pansy – that's for sure

[*Later*. Dutch text: Simon Carmiggelt. Music: Herman van Veen. Album: *In Vogelvlucht*, 1987.]

Epilogue

Oliebollen Festival

"Olly bolly! Oil balls? Fat cakes? Oh, you mean vetkoek." "No, no, oliebollen! Olie because they are fried in oil and bol means ball, you can see that clearly. Look!" That's how Lies responds to visitors who ask about our annual oliebollen festival on the last day of the year.

By four in the afternoon of New Year's Eve, the oliebollen batter is ready, filling Mrs Armstrong's ten litre mixing bowl to the brim. I stir the mixture with a ladle to release the biggest yeast bubbles. "It's time," Lies says and we start carrying our work tools outside. She has written our checklist on a large piece of paper, alongside her recipe. By popular demand, Lies is wearing her Volendamse kant kapje with a red apron. I have tied a red Dutch farmer's handkerchief over my hair.

Our work tables are placed beneath the straw roof of our garage, because the wind usually picks up around five. Eleven years of experience has taught us that it is impossible to cook on a gas stove in the wind. By half past four the two large, heavy-bottomed saucepans are nice and hot, and the first bollen are sizzling in the oil. On the table a colander waits to drain the oil off cooked bollen, alongside a wooden serving platter and a canister for sprinkling icing sugar.

We have two young assistants this year; our visitors Riëtte and Mia are on duty at the ginger beer table. Their table is covered with a tablecloth from Holland, hand embroidered by our friend Dith. She was so proud of it – a red background decorated with white candles and stars. Twenty litres of ginger beer is cooling in the fridge. Suenel's glass tumblers are ready and waiting. Just after five o'clock, the first villagers arrive, initially reticent because nobody wants to be first. "Are we too early?" But fifteen minutes later a jovial group is standing and chatting in front of our home in Breë Street.

"Your olly bolly are so good this year!"

"Yes," says Lies, "but don't eat them too quickly! Remember to examine the shape carefully. What do you see? A little pig or perhaps an elephant? What could this mean for your year ahead?"

We have been cooking for more than an hour. I fill the platter with oliebollen and stroll among the crowd to make sure everyone has sampled at least one or two. Our neighbour Pieter carries another bowlful. The mood is jolly. I greet people I have never seen before, they are probably holiday-makers or guests of residents. They are all excited and amazed that everyone is welcome. People want to make a donation and I tell them that tonight's contributions will go to the Breede Skills-for-life Centre in the village. The donations box is on the ginger beer table.

I look at the happy throng and remember the first New Year's Eve we cooked oliebollen in McGregor, twelve years ago, when we set up our tables in the street in front of Temenos, where we were managing a coffee shop. With time the ritual moved to our street and, without much planning from our side, it's become a fixture on the village calendar. The whole happening, or "event" in today's language, is short but hectic. About one hundred people turn up, entertain themselves and exchange good wishes for the new year. Within two hours all the bollen are fried and eaten and everybody has gone back to their own homes or tourist accommodation.

My first oliebollen feast was at the house of Lies's sister

Corry. This was about fifty years ago in Bloemfontein. In Cape Town, Lies started making them herself, using her mother's recipe which was written down in a small recipe book. With time the number of oliebollen we made increased. It's strange to think that this little recipe has evolved into one that feeds our giant street party.

At eight o'clock friends help us to move the stove and tables back into our kitchen. In a jiffy everything is squeaky clean and back in its place. The street is quiet again. We count the money for the Breede Centre; eight hundred rand on the dot! I remember the anonymous contributions which began appearing on our stoep last week; a packet of sugar, a bag of flour.

....

New Year's Eve 2016. The presence of these glowing young people is a gift to us all: McGregor's Uni-Stars Xmas Band is entertaining the oliebollen festival participants with irresistible dance music. I look at my shed of straw where the last batter is being spooned into the oil. I cannot believe my eyes. Young and old are dancing with spontaneous joy. Breë Street is a picture containing every possible shade and type; a colourful, flavourful composition of Bodorp and Onderdorp in a twirling mass in front of our house. Lies is stepping out in a kind of reel dance with a short brown man. Tourists look on in astonishment. People embrace each other in well wishes for the next year.

And suddenly I see that all my dreams have come true. On their own. This is how it feels to be part of a village, to belong. Warm around the heart.

Glossary

Bokkoms – whole, salted, dried fish (usually mullet) a delicacy of the West Coast

Colok kemenyan – similar to incense or joss sticks

Hotnots (from Hottentots) – a pejorative term first applied to Khokhoi people by Europeans in the 17th century.

Jongetjie – little boy

Koesisters, koeksisters – a sweet confection, sometimes in the shape of a plait, made from a dough that is deep fried and then dipped in syrup.

Koppies (from kopje) – hillocks

Mieliepap – maize porridge

Oliebollen – deep fried batter cakes with raisins and dusted with icing sugar. Distributed among neighbours and eaten on New Year's Eve in the Netherlands. Individual shapes are said to be prophetic about what the New Year holds for the eater.

Ousies – black domestic workers (acquired pejorative connotation)

Riempie – strips of raw hide used to string seats of furniture (also plaited for whips and used as ropes, belts and shoelaces)

Smoortjie – braised food

Stamppot – a traditional Dutch dish made from a combination of potatoes mashed with one or more vegetables

Suurpap – fermented maize porridge

Suurvytjies – edible sour figs of the mesembryanthemaceae

Thuthuzela – (Xhosa) comfort

Tiekiedraai – folk dance; generic terms for a folk dance get-together or volkspele

Volendamse kant kapje – traditional lace and starched cotton bonnet worn by Dutch women for special occasions. Volendam is a district in Holland.

Printed in the United States
By Bookmasters